UNCOVERING THE MYSTERIOUS
WOOLLY MAMMOTH

LIFE AT THE END OF THE GREAT ICE AGE

MICHAEL AND BEVERLY OARD
ILLUSTRATIONS BY BILL LOONEY

First printing: March 2007
Third printing: April 2022

ISBN-13: 978-1-68344-307-0
ISBN-13: 978-1-61458-310-3 (digital)

Library of Congress Catalog Number: 2006937548

Cover Design: Bryan Miller
Interior Design and Layout: Bryan Miller

Please consider requesting that a copy of this volume be purchased by your local library system.

Printed in China.

For information regarding author interviews,
please contact the publicity department at (870) 438-5288.

Please visit our website for other great titles:

www.masterbooks.com

Dedications:

We dedicate this book to our grandchildren:

Jeremiah, Jacob, Elena, Madison, Hailey, Tia, and Launna.

Master
Books®
A Division of New Leaf Publishing Group
www.masterbooks.com

Table of Contents

PART I

PART II

Preface

Life in the Great Ice Age introduced us to Jabeth, his tribe, and the "Beetle-Brow" people as we read about their adventure-filled summer. They hunted woolly mammoths, drove out a cave bear, and celebrated their successes. Jabeth lived at the end of the Ice Age, around 600 years after Noah's flood. By that time, the ice had stopped building. The oceans had cooled to temperatures close to what we have today. The ice sheet was rapidly melting.

Jabeth's tribe originally settled south of the Scandinavian Ice Sheet in central Europe. Big game was abundant. They lived in caves because of their convenience and safety. They hunted and gathered their food using their wits to survive. Stone tools and clever hunting techniques were used to procure food and clothing. Today, Jabeth's people would be considered Cro-Magnons. Their friends, the "Beetle-Brow" tribe, would be called Neanderthals. They also lived in caves. Both people groups were human beings surviving in a challenging environment.

Jabeth and his family lived during the transition from an Ice Age climate to the deglaciation phase. Grandfather remembered the cool summers and mild winters and noticed the change to warmer summers and colder winters. The cooling oceans brought some unexpected events. Less water evaporated. The exposed land became drier. Frequent windstorms gathered huge amounts of dust. Rolling black dust clouds deposited thick layers of wind-blown silt across vast areas of land. The warmer summers caused the edge of the ice sheets to melt. Rivers overflowed their banks and floods swept the lowlands. North of Jabeth's cave home, the "great wall of ice" was melting downward at the rate of about 30 feet per year (10 m/year) and slowly retreating north.

This book continues Jabeth's story but 30 years later. He has become the head of his tribe, replacing his father, Lathan. The story is told through the eyes of Jabeth's 12-year-old son, Eric. During Eric's lifetime, the Scandinavian Ice Sheet disappeared from continental

acquainted with their new neighbors, they learned the woolly mammoths were becoming extinct in Siberia as well as in Europe. The Siberians shared woolly mammoth ivory, while Jabeth's tribe shared seeds and the art of making pottery. The new tribe told Jabeth's people about their adventurous journey as they traveled south from Siberia and west into Europe seeking a better land.

Europe but remained in Scandinavia, exposing the Baltic Sea. The sea is called Lake Baltica in our story. Summers became even warmer and winters colder than when Jabeth was a child. Frequent dust storms of variable intensity continued to blow across the land. The large animals that they used to hunt were becoming either scarce or extinct. Their tribe was growing. It was time to leave the caves behind and develop agriculture and build villages and towns. Civilization began but hunting and gathering continued. The rapid development of agriculture and animal husbandry gradually added to their food supply.

When Jabeth was a child, a trader visited and told them about a far-away land called Siberia. In our story many years later, a strange group of people has moved into their peaceful valley. Jabeth and his tribe discovered they were from Siberia. As they became

Part I

Chapter One

From Caves to Huts

Jabeth, Eric's father, was barely in the lead.

"I won, this time," Jabeth gasped. "It won't be long before you can run faster than me."

Twelve-year-old Eric laughed and said, "That was fun!" Steadying their breath, they looked down the steep trail they had just run up. Nearby, streams hurried nimbly down from the mountain into the river that ran through their valley. Far below them lay their little village. It was early in the summer, so the river was still high. Light rays from the setting sun streamed down through the clouds. The sky was slowly filling with soft shades of rose and orange. A feeling of contentment and joy spread over Eric and Jabeth. Eric knew this was his father's favorite place to go when he needed to be alone. He sensed that his father had invited him here for a special reason.

Jabeth was the leader of the tribe, so he came here often when he had important decisions to make. It was here that he liked to remember the stories his grandfather told him as they sat around the cave fire talking late into the night. The stories reminded him of how the Lord had blessed and guided His people. Lately, he had been thinking about how his father Lathan taught him about life and had prepared him for leadership.

Lathan had moved the tribe into the valley ten summers ago. Not many years later Lathan went the way of his ancestors.

Thinking of his father, Jabeth recalled his first woolly mammoth hunt. He remembered the pride he felt when Lathan had chosen his plan for the hunt.

The hunters used a wall of fire to drive the woolly mammoths over a cliff. Jabeth thought wistfully, Lathan was a good and wise father and leader. Jabeth was hoping he would do as well.

Jabeth knew it was time to start training Eric to become the next leader of their clan. He had been watching his son to see if he had the gift of leadership. He noticed that Eric was protective of the younger children. The older children listened to him. Eric already considered others before he made his decisions. Jabeth decided he would no longer come to his special spot alone. Excitement shivered through Eric as he sensed the reason for Jabeth's invitation.

CAVE LIFE

"Eric, I have been waiting to see if you have the qualities necessary for leadership. I have been pleased with what I have seen. Now that you are twelve years old, it is time to begin your training." Jabeth thought the best way to begin was to teach him how decisions were made. "You must never forget a leader is always accountable to the Creator God and responsible for his tribe's well being. Let me give you an example by telling you how we decided to leave the caves beyond the hills. The caves protected the tribe from bears, saber-toothed tigers, hyenas, and other wild animals. But the caves were cold and damp. My father and grandfather kept the fire at the entrance burning every night. This frightened away the fierce animals that were searching for food and shelter. Sometimes warring tribes traveled through. The caves protected us as we fought to keep our homes and food. But, as our family grew, the caves became too small. It was harder and harder to find enough food for everyone. We needed to find a place that had plenty of game, water, and rich land.

"While we were living in the caves, the weather changed. The winters became colder and lasted longer. The weather changes were so gradual that no one seemed to notice them at first. But, I remember one very cold winter day long ago; the older men were sitting around the fire. They were talking about the time when they were children. They remembered cool summers and mild winters. Back then, the snow was soft and deep and lasted until the early summer. After the snow disappeared, it rained heavily for months. Now winter snow is light and summers are dry.

"Back then, the great wall of ice retreated about thirty feet each summer. The thaw caused the rivers and streams to overflow. Once in a while a dust storm would blow through our area, but soon they came more and more often. Each time they came they were stronger. We would hide in our caves until the storm ended. Gath, Zorak, and some of the others liked to keep busy, so they painted the cave walls or carved on woolly mammoth tusks."

The Mystery of the Disappearing Mammals

Eric and Jabeth suddenly heard a branch crack nearby. Eric reached for his spear and scanned the undergrowth. Eric whispered to his dad, "Maybe it is a woolly mammoth." He then disappeared into the undergrowth and crept quietly to where he had heard the noise. Then, a beautiful elk raised its head and looked at Eric. The elk carried huge antlers that had at least six points.

There were many deer and elk in the valley, but they were hard to hunt because they moved quickly once they were startled. Often hunters would wait for them early in the morning near the streams or high in the mountains. If the men were downwind from them and very quiet, sometimes they were able to get close enough to throw a spear. Eric knew he had to aim well because he wouldn't get a second chance. He slowly raised his arm and let the spear fly. But just as he threw, the animal moved

and the spear dropped to the ground. The stately elk trotted away before Eric could throw again.

Disappointed, he walked back to his father. Jabeth was seated on a boulder, wearing a broad grin. "Did you get your woolly mammoth?"

Eric protested, "If that was a woolly mammoth, I would have killed it."

Jabeth laughed and said, "It would have taken ten grown men and twenty spears just to slow it down. There are better ways to kill a mammoth. We used to run them off cliffs, or if there was a bog nearby, we would drive them into the mud."

Eric remembered, "Didn't you say that Ungar of the Beetle-Brow tribe told us that the woolly mammoths and the other large mammals are disappearing?"

"Yes," answered Jabeth. "Ungar noticed many of the large mammals were becoming scarce. It had been a long time since they had seen a saber-toothed tiger or a woolly rhino. He thought the animals might have starved to death or died in a dust storm."

"I heard him say he thought it was because the grassland was taken over by trees, so there was less for them to eat," said Eric.

"That is probably correct," Jabeth added. "The tigers were dangerous and the hippos mean, so it is safer now for everyone. I miss hunting the woolly mammoth because it could feed us for a moon or more. Now we have to hunt more often and eat smaller game."

The Abandoned Caves

"What made everyone decide it was time to leave the caves?" Eric asked.

Jabeth still remembered the arguments surrounding the decision to leave the caves. "Do you remember what I told you about how we came into this valley?" Jabeth responded. "Your grandfather was convinced that it was best for everyone to find a new home. Gath and Zorak argued that the tribe must stay. They were afraid to leave the safety of the caves. They had lived there south of the ice wall ever since they were born.

"Lathan said we needed more room since the tribe had grown. Gath and Zorak argued that it would be hard to protect the tribe from warring tribes if

Fact Box

1) The ice sheet was retreating rapidly northward during deglaciation.

2) More land became exposed every summer.

3) Deglaciation was windy, with frequent dust storms.

4) The large Ice Age animals commonly went extinct during deglaciation.

5) People rapidly moved out of caves at the end of the Ice Age.

6) Civilization with the building of homes and planting of crops spread rapidly during and after deglaciation.

Fact Box

they left the safety of the caves. Your grandfather had given protection of the tribe much thought. He showed them a miniature rock and clay longhouse that he had designed. 'If we build this longhouse on a hill next to a river, the women and children can run to it when we are in danger. If we have a long mound near it, the men can hide in safety and fight if we have to. We would be as safe as we are in the caves if we build it right.' Lathan asserted.

"Then, it was my turn to speak," Jabeth related. "The tribe listened to my opinion, since some day I was to be their new leader. I remember saying: 'The ice wall melts back more each summer. Each year more land opens up. First grass covers the area up to the ice. And then within a few years trees and bushes fill in where the ice was. The land in front of the ice wall is well watered and filled with game. If we move, we will still be close enough to the caves to run into them if we are in danger.

"I was right, every year the ice continued to melt back, but one year it uncovered a large lake instead of land. The tribe named it Lake Baltica. That year, Lathan made his decision to move from the caves. He had been praying about it since they first discussed the need. Father sent several men to scout for a new home. Everyone prayed that God would lead them to a safe place where we could settle. I learned how important it is to ask God for wisdom before every important decision and to carefully weigh what is best for the tribe.

"My cousin, Baylock, found a broad valley that was protected from the winds and full of deer, elk, wild pigs, and many small animals. It was only two days away, toward the North Star. As far as they could tell, no one else lived there. The valley had a small river running through it and was surrounded by hills. We left the caves one moon later. We journeyed toward the North Star and found the valley to be just as Baylock had said. We chose a site close to the river and built our stone longhouse on the hill for tribal gatherings and protection. Then, each family built their own hut.

"The valley has given us a safe and peaceful home so far, except for when Nabor's band of thieves visit the valley." From their perch they could see smoke curling up from the fire pit near the door of the longhouse. That morning the hunters had killed a red deer. It was roasting on a spit over the fire. Another hunting party had killed some birds and a wild pig. There was to be a celebration tonight thanking the Creator for the successful hunt.

From where Eric sat he could see his younger brother, Ishka, in his little garden. The tribe remembered the story of how Noah's family planted a vineyard after they left the ark and tried to grow their favorite wild grains and legumes. In the fertile valley floor they grew lentils and grain. After they had settled in the valley, Gath had traded for seeds with a tribe from another valley upriver. Even with the produce, the tribe still gathered berries, nuts, and roots in the fall. Often they would cast their nets for fish. They gathered enough food to dry and store for the next winter. Usually, the hunters found only small game, but the tribe always seemed to have enough food. They never forgot to thank God for the many gifts that He gave them.

Chapter Two

The Great Escape

BARE SURVIVAL IN NORTHERN SIBERIA

Icy winds had been blowing steadily for several moons. It seemed the relentless wind stopped only long enough to catch its breath before it began again. The sound reminded Tungus of wolves howling. It set a person's nerves on edge. His small, lonely village huddled close to the vast expanse of ice that was once Lake Arctica in northern Siberia. Their yurts dotted the landscape, looking a lot like mole heaps. Smoke from their hearths was quickly blown away by the harsh wind. Inside, Tungus' family wrapped their furs tighter around them.

Recently, the winds had grown stronger, and whipped up dirt from the plains and dropped it against their homes, rocks, and trees, and sometimes even buried an animal. As carefully as Tungus and his family tried to keep their home tight, dust filtered in between the furs that lined their hut. The family's reindeer were kept inside a rock shed so they could breathe more easily. They were as restless as Tungus and his family.

While they waited for the winds to stop, they entertained each other, telling stories and playing games. Tungus' father, Yakut, told of when the coastland was filled with wildflowers and grass and about the animals Tungus' grandfather Zuda hunted. At that time there were many mammoth herds, and the bogs had not yet formed. But, when Yakut was a boy, one winter the ground froze so deeply that during the summer only the topsoil melted. Gullies filled up with meltwater. The topsoil and water made a thick sticky mud that did not drain because of the frozen soil beneath. Grass grew around the bogs, luring unsuspecting animals into them. The hunters were very clever and used the bogs to their advantage. They waited for the summer bogs to develop in the lowlands and used them to trap woolly mammoths. Later around the campfire, it was great fun watching father as he acted out the hunt. His face glowed with the memory. Then Yakut's face changed as he told him that the woolly mammoths were disappearing. Tungus had noticed them decrease in his short lifetime of 12 years. The cold didn't seem to bother the mammoths too much, but when the snow was deep, it was hard for them to find enough water and grass. This year they saw many die and become covered with blowing dust.

The winters were so cold, windy, and long that Tungus' family had been talking about moving in the direction away from the North Star. There they would find more grass for their animals and better hunting. Most of the other tribes had already moved away. They followed the horses and bison as they traveled away from the North Star up the Lena River. Far south there was a giant long lake they called Lake Baikal. Late that night, while they were sleeping, the winds finally stopped and a penetrating cold settled around the village.

Shivering, Tungus gazed over the vast landscape. The soft light of the midday sun gave the mighty Lena River a silvery hue. The late winter ice still covered the Lena River and Lake Arctica. A thick layer of dirty snow blanketed the land for as far as he could see. Tungus had never seen so much wind and blowing dirt before. The weather was so bad that even the hunters did not dare to go outside. Food supplies were getting low.

LEAVE OR DIE

Tungus felt a shiver of excitement in the air. He remembered that tonight all of the men from the village were going to have a meeting. The meetings usually meant fun and games, but not tonight. He had heard whispers that maybe something big would be decided. The women were muttering among themselves that the men had to do something soon. The dried meat was dwindling, and no one had spotted a woolly mammoth for some time. The fishermen found it difficult to ice fish in the short time between dust storms. The sun was becoming higher in the direction away from the North Star but it would be several moons before new grass would grow and the ice broke on the Lena River. The tribe feared the food would not last until then.

Men representing the rest of the families in their little village began filling Tungus' yurt. Yakut was a strong man, well-known for his honesty and wisdom. The family depended on him for so much, yet even he looked worried. Uncle Barash sat in the corner without his usual smile. Tungus' older brother, Kolyma, and grandfather Zuda quietly took their places with the others around the fire. Ama, Tungus' mother, wordlessly served koumiss, fermented reindeer milk. Since there was so little room in the yurt, the other women stayed home with the children.

Many nights before, the men had talked late into the night trying to decide whether to move or whether to wait for summer. The situation was getting desperate. As the meeting proceeded, Yakut was the first to speak: "Long ago our ancestors traveled to this place. There was good hunting and plenty of food for all of us to eat. Since then winters have become colder and longer. The mists no longer rise from Lake Arctica. The ice gods have covered the great waters. The sun god hides his face from us. We no longer feel warm breezes on our faces. Few of the horses, bison, woolly rhinoceroses, and other animals remain. Most of the woolly mammoths have died because there is not enough grass for them to eat in the winter. Some have drowned in the great floods that flowed down from the melting mountain ice caps. Last summer nomads said that if we follow the Lena River away from the North Star, we would come close to a huge, long lake. There the summers are longer and the winters less cold. It is time we follow the way of the animals until we find a new home."

Grandfather Zuda agreed and said, "Some in our tribe are too old to travel such a distance. If only one or two families stay, there may be enough food to last until it warms up, but there are too many of us for all to stay."

"It is either move or starve!" Kolyma blurted out what they all knew. They talked late into the night, worried about the dangers of the journey.

Finally Barash took his turn to speak, saying, "The ice in the river is still thick. It will be melting in several moons. We can take our sledges on the ice of the river and travel fast. We must leave between dust storms. We can reach the great forest where the dust does not blow as much."

Yakut said, "But, if we wait too long, it will become too dangerous to travel on the ice. The ice will break and crush our sleds, or we will fall into the water and drown. We must go when the wind slows, and the ice is still strong." Everybody nodded in agreement.

In the days that followed, the winds seemed angry and blew even harder, but while it raged the families were very busy preparing for their long journey. They had to travel light. The reindeer, dogs, and men had to pull the sleds. They could only pack their most needed possessions.

Yakut made a sled using larch wood he had collected the previous summer from the mountains. He cut strips of leather for securing their belongings. He hoped that by leaning several sleds against each other and covering them with hides, they could be used as shelters. They had to wear all of their clothes to further lighten the sleds. The men had to walk most of the way. They gathered their hunting javelins, scrapers, knives, needles, ropes made of hides, and nets for fishing. They packed only enough dried fish and meat to help them when they were unable to kill animals or catch fish along the way. They packed berries, roots, and most important of all, the sacred fire holder. They carefully packed woolly mammoth tusks for trading.

SLEDDING TO LAKE BAIKAL

Tungus was impatient to start this new adventure. Day after day passed and the winds kept blowing. The sun rose higher and higher in the sky, away from the North Star. They would have to leave soon or it would be too dangerous.

Finally, one morning Tungus woke up to a strange silence. At first he didn't understand why it was so quiet. Then he noticed that the sides of his yurt were not shaking. The winds must have stopped in the middle of the night. Tungus saw his father and grandfather sitting by the fire.

Grandfather said gravely, "It is time. You must go this morning; we don't know how long we have before the next storm." Tungus knew to not interrupt so he listened intently. "Lamut and his family offered to stay with us. His broken leg has not healed enough for the journey, but soon he can hunt and care for us," said Grandfather. "His sons will be able to hunt with him." Two other families also decided to stay. Tungus was sad. He didn't know that Grandfather Zuda would not be traveling with them.

Everyone helped Tungus, Yakut, and the rest of the families take down their yurts and pack. They gave many gifts to each other and many words of advice. Grandfather handed Tungus his bear claw amulet. "I want you to keep the amulet. The bear god will help you become a mighty hunter."

Tungus struggled to keep his emotions from overflowing. "I am sorry you cannot come with us.

I hope that some day we can come back for you. I will never forget you."

The clan let them take some tamed reindeer to use for milk and as pack animals. Many dogs were selected to pull the sledges. Wolf, Tungus' dog, was useful as a watchdog and could help with the sledges, so he was allowed to go too.

After a few mishaps, the loads on the sledges were adjusted. The dogs' excitement and the people's loud good-byes were deafening. Many tears were shed that day because most knew they would never see each other again. They moved forward to the edge of the river with Yakut taking the lead. Flakes of ice filled the air and sparkled in the morning sun. The frozen river lay before them like a white ribbon as far as Tungus could see. It looked so peaceful. Last summer the river was a muddy, raging torrent as melting glaciers in the mountains rushed their load of water and dirt into Lake Arctica. Tungus had watched it from the safety

Fact Box

1) Thick wind blown silt, called loess, covers large areas of northern Siberia.

2) Snow and ice built up in the mountains only, the lowlands were unglaciated.

3) As the Ice Age progressed, winters became colder and summers warmer.

4) The Arctic Ocean was unfrozen until the end of the Ice Age.

5) There was little permafrost in Siberia at the beginning of the Ice Age.

6) Permafrost increased during the middle and end of the Ice Age.

Fact Box

of a hill as the discolored water fanned out over the top of Lake Arctica. Now he was trudging up the frozen river to a land known only by the tales others told.

The first day went by without any major mishaps. The winds remained light, the ice held, and the sledges swooshed forward at a fast clip, pulled by the reindeer and dogs and guided by the men. Tungus' little brother, Zuda, named after his grandfather, and his mother, Ama, rode a reindeer. Zuda was so closely wrapped to his mother that he could hardly be seen. A leather butter churn bounced alongside of them. By the time they stopped, a small round ball of butter would fill the bottom of the churn. Tungus trotted alongside the sleds until he was too tired. Then he was allowed to ride. It was so cold that he preferred walking. By dinner the first evening everyone was very tired and hungry.

Marak and some other men went out to hunt horses. They had seen the horses before stopping to camp. The men set up the shelters as the women prepared the fire for cooking. The fishermen chopped a hole in the ice and hooked enough fish for dinner. Tungus and his friends staked the reindeer near the temporary yurts and milked them. After the fishermen had eaten, they caught more fish so the dogs could eat. The dogs needed to be strong; they had so far to travel. Each person had a job to do. Everyone's work was appreciated and needed to keep everybody alive and healthy. Marak and the men came back late from their hunt. They were unable to find the horses.

Thin Ice

Each day brought new wonders and new dangers for Tungus and his tribe. The mountains and hills that lined the river were dotted with scrub larch. Bison hid in their canyons and big-horned sheep were spotted high on the cliffs. Hunting was difficult since there were so few trees; it was hard to sneak up on the animals. They often relied on the fish they caught.

Tungus and his family had been traveling for several days. It was three days before a dust storm engulfed the travelers. They hid in their hastily set up yurts until the storm finally ended.

Traveling on the river assured they would not become lost when they did travel during a dust storm. One day seemed to run into another. Temperatures gradually warmed as they entered the great forest. They continued away from the North Star for many days through the great forest. Then one clear day, Tungus noticed along the banks of the river colorful butterflies and flies swirling around puddles of melting snow. During the night, they heard the Lena River groan as ice chunks cracked and rubbed against each other.

The last day on the river was a day etched in all of their memories. Yakut, Tungus, and the rest of the families broke camp. Yakut learned that ahead the river ran through a narrow canyon. Yakut, Barash, and Marak decided to risk one more day on the ice. If they were careful, the ice would hold long enough for them to make it through the narrows. The ice up ahead was shaded by the mountains. It appeared to be firm enough to support them. They carefully packed their sleds, tightly wrapping their belongings. The dogs yelped with excitement, anticipating the adventure ahead of them. Yakut ordered each sled to be separated by a large distance, in case one broke through the ice. Yakut led, taking Tungus and Marak with him.

The dogs leapt forward as Yakut ably steered them around small cracks in the ice. They swooshed up the river as fast as the dogs could run. By late afternoon they could see the end of the canyon. Suddenly a loud crack erupted beneath them and a long chunk of ice tilted downward as water gushed into the crack. The dogs pulled forward with all of their strength. Yakut shouted orders to the dogs. The sled slipped toward the bubbling water in the middle of the river. Wolf was in the lead. Tungus and Yakut pushed with all of their strength to help the dogs up the wedge. The dogs scrambled and slipped. For a moment it looked as though all was lost, but Wolf made it to the top of the ice and dropped onto the solid ice, pulling the rest of the dogs along with him.

The rest of the sleds quickly headed toward shore. When the danger was over, Tungus' legs and arms felt like rubber. Everyone was congratulating him for saving them and the sled. His father said, "This day you have become a man. You were strong in the face of danger." He raised Tungus' arm and all cheered him. Tungus was very glad to have made his father proud.

For a half moon Tungus remembered walking alongside the river, struggling through tangled undergrowth and around deadfall in the great forest. Then, they left the river, heading away from the North Star Finally, Lake Baikal glimmered in the distance. The sun reflected brightly off the melting ice. When they stepped on the shore of the lake, Ama tasted the water and declared it good. The scouts had spotted many kinds of large and small animals. Everyone broke out in cheers. Their journey was over. This was the lake they were seeking.

Chapter Three

The Rescue of the Siberian Tribe

Baylock was on his way to meet a hunting expedition when he decided to see how his new friend Yakut and his family were faring. A week ago he had found them camping up the river. Yakut welcomed him, and they did some trading. He enjoyed spending the afternoon visiting.

When Baylock was a short way off, he saw his old enemy, Nabor, talking loudly to Yakut. Nabor's band of thieves was lurking in the surrounding trees.

Fortunately, Nabor did not notice him. He knew it would be only a short time before they attacked his new friends. Baylock rushed back to the village to get help.

Jabeth, Eric, and Ishka were target practicing with spears next to the longhouse. "Nabor is threatening the tribe I told you about." Baylock was clearly worried. "Hurry, they are about a mile up the river. They don't stand a chance against Nabor and his band of thieves."

Jabeth blew on his horn. The fighting men quickly gathered in front of the lodge with their weapons in hand. Jabeth hoped the robbers would hear the ram's horn and run, but if they didn't, his tribe would be ready. Jabeth quickly told his warriors that Nabor was in their territory.

Baylock spoke to the gathering men, "I met Yakut and his clan one week ago. They said they came from the direction of the rising sun and have traveled for many moons. Their tribal clothes are different from any I have seen. They are very worn and tattered. The women and children are very tired. They had mammoth ivory and beads they wanted to use for trade. So I traded them ivory for food. There are not many of them. They are helpless against Nabor and his troublemakers."

Jubal declared, "Nabor has gotten away with stealing and killing for too long. Every year more men join him. Sooner or later we will have to fight them. It is better to fight now when there are more of us than them." The rest of the men nodded their heads in approval. Jabeth let out a war whoop and the rest of the men raised their spears and yelled in agreement.

THE RESCUE

Eric and his brother Ishka were not allowed to fight because they were not strong enough yet. So they hid in some bushes and watched with Gath, who was too old to fight. Eric could see that their warriors held the advantage of surprise. The robbers hadn't heard Jabeth's horn or the tribe approaching, because the women and children were screaming and crying. As Jabeth quietly approached, he saw five men tied up under a large spruce tree. One of them had blood streaming down the side of his face. The robbers were tearing through their belongings, trying to find ivory and anything else of value. The women huddled together, trying to protect their children.

Jabeth and his men yelled a blood-curdling war cry and rushed toward the robbers. The surprise and fierce look of Jabeth's men had its effect. Nabor realized they were outnumbered. They were terrified. He recognized Jabeth as he swung his battle-ax in fierce and terrifying fury. Jabeth ducked as Nabor's ax flew over his head. When Nabor realized that he was outnumbered and that Jabeth was still agile enough to outmaneuver him, he yelled retreat. The thieves ran rather than fight a losing battle. Jabeth was glad. He really didn't want anyone to be hurt or killed. Jabeth knew that if his men looked fierce enough and made enough noise, the enemy often would lose heart and run. Hand-to-hand combat takes great courage. He knew that one of these days Nabor would not run. Then there would eventually be a fight to see who would have control of the valley.

Eric ran up to Jabeth. He was very proud of his father. Eric surveyed the damage the thieves had done. Jabeth and his men quickly untied the men and checked on their wounds. The robbers had torn through their packs but not much was missing. Most of their ivory had already been traded. In Nabor's rush to get away, his men had dropped much of their booty on the trail. Even though the battle was over, the women were still frightened and the children crying. They were not sure whether Eric's tribe was friend or enemy.

Eric held out his hand to comfort one of the smallest boys. The boy's dark eyes looked at him with suspicion. Eric gently talked to him. The women noticed Eric's kindness. They calmed down and waited to see what would happen next.

Eric smiled and brushed the dirt off of the boy's clothes. The boy looked up and said, "I, Zuda," as he pointed to himself.

"I am Eric," said Eric as he pointed to himself.

Gath had been watching the battle from a distance. When the fighting ended, he joined Baylock and approached Yakut. When Yakut recognized his new friend, he smiled broadly. It was then he was sure the tribe was rescued. Fortunately, no one was seriously hurt.

Gath was the translator for Eric's tribe. He used the language of the traders to tell Yakut and his tribe that Nabor was their enemy too. As was the custom, Gath then waited for Jabeth to speak. Jabeth invited the wandering tribe to come to their village for safety and to bind up their wounds. He was surprised to learn that they were from very far away, from the direction of the rising sun and the North Star — the land of Siberia.

NEW FRIENDS

Eric noticed there was a boy about his age among the strangers. He wore a bear claw amulet around his neck and was dressed in soft furs. Eric walked up and introduced himself. "I am Eric," he said and pointed to himself.

The other boy said, "Tungus." Both of them smiled.

Eric and Tungus walked together to the village. Eric knew a little sign language and tried to talk to Tungus. Every once in while Tungus nodded his head, as if he understood. Eric motioned for Tungus to follow him. "I will show you our village," Eric said excitedly. Tungus seemed to understand and followed him. Wolf trotted beside his master.

Eric showed Tungus his house and Ishka's garden. Tungus was very interested in the garden, since he had never seen one back in Siberia. The vegetables had come up one moon ago. Eric showed Tungus how he and Ishka had planted seeds and watered them. With the sunshine and warmth, the plants grew. He pulled an onion and ate one. Then he pulled one up for his new friend to taste. Tungus took a bite and grimaced. He had never tasted an onion before.

Next, Eric took Tungus to Zorak's garden and showed him the lentil and barley. He showed him the goats that his brother had tamed. Together they gathered the goats and walked them back to their pen. Tungus was surprised to see that goats could be tamed and milked. He liked petting them. They were a lot like having dogs. Eric used sign language to explain how the goats were tamed by Ishka, Eric's ten-year-old brother, alternately pointing to the goats and Ishka. "One day a few years ago, while Ishka was playing in the forest, he found a baby

goat. He felt sorry for it and cared for the little one. Everyone thought it was funny when the goat followed him around as if he were its mother. When the goat grew up, they found that taming a goat was useful for milk. Before long, Ishka had gathered and tamed several more. He had a gentle touch with animals. This encouraged the tribe to try to tame other animals."

Eric was not sure how much Tungus understood, but Tungus' nod indicated that he caught the gist of the story. "Let me show you the longhouse. I think you'll like it," Eric said, pointing toward the stone structure sitting on the small hilltop. Ishka

joined them. The boys walked through the giant doors. Tungus' eyes were huge as they took in the many sights and smells. The memory of many wonderful hunts lined the walls. There were bear pelts, including the giant cave bear that Gath, Lathan, Ungar, and others had killed. Deer and elk horns hung high in the rafters. They still had a few woolly mammoth tusks hung along the walls. Their many treasures spoke of adventures, friends, and hunts. The longhouse was the tribe's gathering place. It also told the story of Eric's people. Carvings made of wood and ivory decorated one wall. Eric promised to tell him the story of his people later. Tungus

1) Some tribes or families were peaceful but others were warlike.

2) Once people left caves, they rapidly developed agriculture and animal husbandry.

3) Hunting smaller game replaced woolly mammoth hunts at the end of the Ice Age.

4) Mammoth ivory was commonly carved during the Ice Age.

5) People living in the Ice Age made very nice stone spear points.

6) Stone tools can be sharp and very efficient at butchering animals.

promised to do the same. Their talking came to an end when Eric's mother called them to help haul water. It was time for him to help the women prepare dinner. It was a huge job, and all of the children were needed to help.

THE WILD PIG HUNT

Yakut, Tungus, and the rest of the tribe slept well that night. They had been exhausted from the fight and rested well on happily full stomachs. Suddenly, Baylock shook Yakut awake. It was early morning and the sun had just risen. Baylock asked in sign language if Yakut and some of his men would like to join a hunt. He had been out scouting at first light and spotted several wild pigs in a meadow not too far from the village. They had to act fast. At first, Jabeth thought he had enough men for the hunt. However, he soon realized that he needed more men. With more

hunters, it would be easier to flush the pigs out into the clearing on the other side of the meadow. Tungus saw the excited look in the men's faces as they described how they planned to kill the animals. Eric soon came into the tent. Yakut and Jabeth had gathered the men. Jabeth used a stick to draw his plan in the dirt so everyone would know what their role would be in this hunt.

Jabeth sent Baylock to see if the boars had moved. Tungus and Eric were allowed to go with the men, but had to keep their distance. Jabeth, with Yakut and his men, formed a line on the far end of the meadow and waited for the pigs to see them. Boars often charge men instead of running away, so hunting them is dangerous.

Jabeth heard a rustle. Barash quietly sneaked around some bushes and started beating the grass. As they had feared, one of the animals charged them. Barash turned and ran. The angry animal was huge and had two horns protruding from each side of his mouth. Jabeth saw that Barash was in trouble and threw his spear. It missed. Fortunately, Kolyma was near and threw another spear. The wild boar squealed and fell to the ground, none too soon.

Baylock and Jubal found two more boars. They beat the bushes and yelled loudly. This time the animals were startled enough to run toward the meadow where Marak, Yakut, and the other tribesmen were waiting. Their hearts were beating hard as they readied their spears. The pigs were big and fat and by this time very angry. Marak and Yakut drew back their spears. They threw straight and true — a sign of many years of practice. Two more animals were killed. Jabeth let out a victory whoop, and the others loudly joined in. Everyone was excited about their success and relieved that no one was injured.

The three boars were tied to poles. One man carried each end of the pole with the boar in the middle. Eric and Tungus danced around the animals and the straining men all the way back to camp. The women and children excitedly ran up, curious about the hunt and eager to hear the story. A pit for roasting the pigs had been dug and lined with hot stones while the men hunted. The younger children had gathered fragrant grass to line the pit. The women and children worked together to make ready for the feast as the men visited outside Jabeth's hut. Occasionally they were called on to help with some of the heavier work. It took most of the day to cook the pigs and prepare the other food. Finally, all was ready. The tables were heaped with succulent pig, grouse, and duck. The lentils and grains were boiled with onions. Some grains were mixed with fat and fried into cakes. Everyone was able to eat his or her fill. Laughter filled the air as the adults watched the children's antics while they tried to communicate with each other. Later, the men and older children had spear-throwing contests.

Chapter Four

Siberia – Once a Land of Plenty

The setting sun filled the horizon with shades of red, violet, pink, and orange. As darkness descended, the festivities moved into the stone lodge. It was tradition to sit around the fire and tell stories far into the night. The light keepers lit the torches and placed them in wall holders. Everyone crowded in; the tribal lodge barely held the two tribes. The women and children pressed against the outer wall as they eagerly waited to hear the Siberians' story. Jabeth, Yakut, and the other men formed the inner circle. Eric and Tungus were allowed to sit with the men since they were the tribal leaders' sons. Ania, Eric's mother, and her friend Anjui made sure that everyone's cup was filled with berry juice or goat's milk. A murmur of excitement rippled through the crowd. They were eager to hear about Siberia and their adventurous journey. Many also wondered if the newcomers knew anything more about what had happened to the woolly mammoths. Ever since Jabeth and the others had learned the tribe came from Siberia, their curiosity had been stirred. Yakut was their spokesman and Gath translated. By now Gath had become good at understanding Yakut. He used traders' sign language and soon they shared new words.

EARLY SIBERIAN WANDERINGS

When the talking began, a great hush fell over the crowd as everyone strained to hear. Gath talked to Yakut. Their hands were moving quickly. When they had trouble understanding each other, one or the other would use a stick to draw a picture in the sand. Kolyma and Barash added details. Then Jabeth asked Yakut, with Gath translating, "How did your tribe come to live in Siberia? We hear it is a cold and miserable land."

Gath listened to Yakut for what seemed like a long time. Gath seemed to be very excited. Then Gath spoke, "Yakut says that long, long ago there was a great flood over the whole land. Eight

people were saved in a boat. He says that after the flood their ancestors settled in a land of two rivers. They grew many types of food and had many children. Eventually they built a city. The king, named Nimrod, demanded that everyone work on a high tower. He wanted to build it so high that if another flood came they would not drown. As they worked on it, anger and confusion arose. Soon, they were not able to understand each other's language or agree on anything. The fighting continued until, in disgust, most of the families left. Each went a different way, so they would not meet each other and start fighting again. Their family at first traveled toward the rising sun and then turned toward the North Star. They followed the woolly

mammoth, bison, horses, and many other large animals. Finally, they could go no farther. They had reached a giant salty lake."

"That must be Lake Arctica — they lived next to giant, salty Lake Arctica!" Gath interjected. "Many moons ago, a wandering tribe passed by our caves. They told us about a lake that is very far toward the North Star and the rising sun."

Gath continued Yakut's story. "Lake Arctica was once a warm lake. Every morning mists used to rise from the water. Trees and bushes and grass lined the coast. Beautiful flowers dotted the landscape. It was home for many different animals.

"Yakut says a huge river empties into the salty lake. He said his ancestors named it the

Lena River. To the distant east, high hills rose above the surrounding plain. They called them the New Siberian hills. When their ancestors first arrived at Lake Arctica, Siberian winters were mild and wet and the summers were cool. Plenty of grass grew. The many types of animals were well fed. Huge herds of woolly mammoths, horses, woolly rhinoceros, bison, antelope, musk oxen, moose, big horn sheep, and reindeer grazed on the grassland. Many wolves, cave lions, foxes, wolverines, ferrets, badgers, and beavers lived there. Hunting was good. They lived next to Lake Arctica for many generations, west of the New Siberian hills. Siberia was a land of plenty. It was not a miserable place to live. Each year the shore of the lake kept moving toward the North Star, as if it was drying up. Every year the snow became deeper and deeper in the mountains and eventually glaciers filled the mountain valleys."

The howl of wolves cut through the air and the room suddenly became silent. Tungus broke the silence by talking to Yakut. "Father, please can I tell them about the time when my grandfather was attacked by lions?"

Yakut looked at his son and said to Gath, "The howl of wolves reminds Tungus of a story that his grandfather used to tell him." Gath encouraged him to tell his story.

Tungus began, gesturing with his hands at times and other times writing in the sand. Gath translated. "My grandfather and his three brothers were out hunting one cool summer day. Hunting had been poor all week. They were next to a small stream that empties into the Lena River. It was a marshy area filled with underbrush and grass. They spotted a small herd of moose. Moose were rare in those parts, because all the tribes relished the meat. They are easy to hunt compared to most other animals. So they were very excited.

"Grandfather and his brothers crept quietly through the low bushes where the moose were grazing. They spotted a majestic bull moose with huge antlers. He was separated a little from the herd. They very slowly crept toward it, careful not to make the slightest noise. Just as the moose raised its head, Grandfather signaled. The men threw their spears. The moose spun around, ran a short distance, and fell to the ground. Grandfather had a perfect throw, right to the heart. He was glad because he did not want to cause the animal to suffer. The other moose heard the noise and ran away. The tribe had plenty of meat and huge moose antlers to remind themselves of the hunt.

"Grandfather and his brothers were cleaning out the animal, when they heard a low growl coming from downstream. A few days before, Grandfather's brother, Sincar, had spotted some cave lions lurking in the area. They looked around but didn't spot anything. The men butchered the animal as quickly as they could and kept alert in case there were cave lions nearby. Then they heard another growl. This time it came from upstream and closer. Grandfather and the men knew for sure that two or more cave lions were sneaking up to steal their kill. They readied their spears, determined to defend themselves and their moose.

"Suddenly, two large lions stood on opposite sides of the clearing. Their teeth were frightening. They gave a low growl and slowly circled the meadow. The lions wanted the moose meat, but the men were determined to keep it. Their tribe was hungry. Then one of the lions charged. Grandfather threw his spear but missed. Sincar held his spear. The lion leapt at him, and Sincar sunk the spear into the lion's neck. It screamed in rage and fell to Sincar's side. The second lion stopped, just out of range of the spears. Grandfather retrieved his spear. Then it roared and lunged at Grandfather. He held onto his spear and stabbed it as the lion lunged at him. The first lion was only wounded. It raised itself up and wobbled toward the men. Grandfather's back was turned toward the lion. It took a swipe at Grandfather. Its razor-sharp claws slashed deeply into his arm. Sincar picked up a large rock and threw it at the lion. He missed. Then he quickly threw another rock and hit it on the head. This time he didn't miss, but it only made the lion angry. Then the lion made a final weak charge. The other men speared it again, and the lion lay motionless. By then, the second lion had sneaked away badly wounded. Grandfather's arm was bleeding heavily. Sincar and the rest of Grandfather's brothers

looked for spider webs to stop the bleeding. They found enough to make a small poultice. Sincar placed it over Grandfather's wound. He placed a leaf over it and wrapped it tightly with a strip of leather. The men helped Grandfather back to camp, while the rest of the men finished butchering the moose. All of the able-bodied tribesmen were called to help bring the meat home. The antlers were very heavy and would be very useful. Grandfather would often show us his scar and tell us of his battle with the cave lions over the moose."

As Gath finished telling Tungus' story, the children were wide eyed. Tungus' story reminded Eric of Gath's battle with the cave bear and the wound that Gath so proudly displayed.

The Great Flood and the Tower of Rebellion

Jabeth spoke while Gath translated: "We too have heard of the Great Flood from our ancestors. We also know the building of the tower caused great division and fighting."

Eric's eyes lit up. "Can I tell our story, father?"

Jabeth remembered how his father, Lathan, and Grandfather used to let him tell the stories when he was a boy. Jabeth had carefully taught the stories of the past to Eric and had him repeat them to make sure he had it right. "Go ahead, son," Jabeth said.

Eric enthusiastically began and Gath carefully translated to Yakut and his tribe. "Your story sounds very similar to ours. Our ancestors told about a worldwide flood that happened long ago. They spoke of a Creator God who judged the earth because all the people were evil in all of

on a high mountain. When the ground was dry enough, God opened the door of the boat. Then, God made the rainbow as a sign that He will never again send another worldwide flood. The animals left the boat, multiplied, and spread to the four corners of the earth. The people moved from the mountains of Ararat to find land for growing plants. They settled in a rich valley between two great rivers. God had instructed them to have many children and spread over all of the earth, but instead they remained in the land of two rivers.

"As time went on and people multiplied, they built a tower and forgot the Creator God's instructions. They disobeyed Him. They even worshiped the sun, the moon, the stars, animals, and other things that they could see. God knew that their evil choices would cause them to destroy themselves. So, He caused the language of each family group to be confused. They spread across the land. Our family traveled toward the North Star, but soon we turned toward the setting sun. We have been very careful to not forget the Creator God."

Eric continued, "Several tribes have stumbled upon our valley as they looked for a better place to live. Traders have paddled down our river. All have told similar stories. They remember the great Flood. They also think that they were the only tribe that was saved from the floodwaters. They have added strange stories and have other gods that they believed caused the Flood. We believe all of the tribes of the earth came from those eight ancestors on the great boat, because the great Flood covered all the lands."

Yakut looked puzzled. Then he spoke to Gath and said, "I vaguely remember my great uncle talking about an unknown God who made everything. But, our tribe worships what we can see: the sun, moon, the stars, and fire. We ask the sun and the earth and the mountain gods to help us. The sun brings warmth, the fire god does too, and the earth gives us good hunting. But in Siberia, our gods abandoned us." Yakut wanted to learn more about the God

their ways. Only one man obeyed God. His name was Noah. God told him to build a very large boat to save the people who would obey Him. It was large enough to hold two of every kind of animal. When the time was right, the animals came to the boat, but only eight people believed God. There was Noah and his wife, along with Noah's three sons and their wives. One of those sons was Japheth, our distant ancestor.

"After the Creator God closed the door of the ark, the wind, rain, and fountains of the great deep came. The water of the ocean covered the entire earth. All of the land animals died. Only those that stayed inside the boat lived. All of the people died except those in the boat. After a very long time, the ark landed

who made everything. He decided he would ask Jabeth when they were alone.

METAL TOOLS

Kolyma pointed to a metal ax that hung from the rafters of the lodge. He asked Gath where such a tool came from. Eric understood the question and was eager to have his father answer it. He loved to hear his father's rich voice and listen to his stories. "Tell him the story of the time you went hunting and brought back rocks instead of meat," Eric said.

Jabeth laughed and then began. "It was a bad day for hunting. I couldn't find even a mouse. Then, when I crossed a stream I saw something sparkle in the sun," Jabeth said. "When I was young, I heard stories handed down by the ancestors. They said that at the Tower of Rebellion people melted shiny rocks in a hot fire. They then poured the liquid into molds. This is how they made tools. Those tools lasted longer and had many more uses than the ones we chip out of rock. He said the knowledge of making metal tools was lost as they spread from the Tower of Rebellion. Many of our family thought metal tools were just a fairytale. But, I often dreamed about finding the shiny rocks and learning the way to melt and shape them.

"There were many sparkling rocks in the stream. I gathered them from the stream and stuffed them into my pack. When I returned from my hunting trip, my friends teased me. They did not believe the stories about tools that never wore out. They wanted food, not rocks! I was so excited about the shiny rocks that I didn't care. As soon as I could, I built a very hot fire. I knew how to make the fire extra hot by tunneling under the hearth and blowing air in through a hollow bone.

"Sure enough, the shiny part melted. It took me a while to discover how to gather enough metal. I very carefully poured the liquid into a hole in a rock. When it was cool, I chipped away the rock. I discovered that the metal was brittle and broke easily. I kept experimenting, hoping to find a way to make it strong enough to be useful. One day I accidentally dropped some charcoal from the fire pit into the shiny liquid. It was a happy accident because I discovered that it made the metal stronger. After much effort, I learned that the constant reheating and pounding gave the metal strength. The more I worked it, the stronger it was. I shaped hammers and knives that were strong and tough. My success encouraged the tribe to not be afraid to try new ideas and not to let teasing stop them. We do not have many of these tools because it is a long and hard process that needs many rocks."

Yakut asked Jabeth if he would teach his tribe how to make metal tools that never wear out.

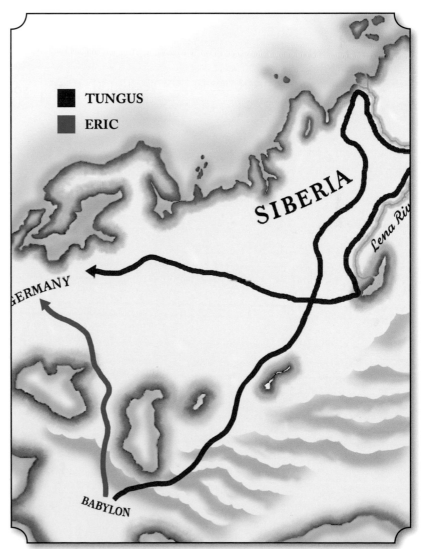

Chapter Five

On the Edge of Survival

The night wore on. A few briefly yawned, but most were wide eyed, listening to the exchange of stories between the two tribes. "Tell us why you left Siberia and how you journeyed so far to our valley," Jabeth asked through Gath.

SIBERIA — A DEATH TRAP

Gath translated their story, "Our people lived close to Lake Arctica. Many animals congregated close to the lake, especially the woolly mammoths. Summers were becoming dangerous farther inland. Bogs grew larger and larger and dust storms swept the land. The animals that could not survive these changes moved close to the coast. The winters were warmer there. More food and water was available for them. Then the coastal area changed too.

"Each year the water rose higher on Lake Arctica. We had to keep moving our village away from the North Star. We think that Lake Arctica was filling with water from the melting ice and snow that came down from the mountains. During the summers the Lena swelled and became a muddy, roaring torrent. You could see the waters as they fanned out over Lake Arctica. We stayed away from the river until it fell in the autumn. In the winter, the ice on the Lena River grew very thick.

"Lake Arctica grew colder and colder each year. The mists no longer rose. The winters became longer and were colder and dryer. Winds blew the snow off of areas of grass so the animals were able to find food. Then the grass that the mammoths and other animals ate slowly disappeared. Bogs gradually replaced the good grass. We were happy to see the summers grow warmer but they were very dry. Huge dust storms swept the coastland too. The larger dust storms filled some of the bogs. So, the growth of the bogs was slow. But, more and more bogs developed until most of the flat land was filled with them.

"Sometimes woolly mammoths and other animals would accidentally wander into the bogs. Occasionally, an animal would get stuck and couldn't get out. As the summer bogs grew larger, the animals that liked to burrow deep into the earth, the badgers and ferrets, disappeared. They could not dig in the frozen ground or live in the soggy topsoil so they left for a warmer land. The huge herds of antelope that ran free all over Siberia grew smaller and smaller."

Jabeth asked, "What made you finally decide to leave Siberia?"

Gath translated and Yakut continued, "The dust storms made living impossible. Every year they blew over the plains. They were especially bad in spring but would come at any time of the year. The blowing dust filled many of the bogs. But the next summer there were more bogs. Gradually, less and less grass grew in the plains. Some tribes left the plains of Siberia, but we stayed. We fished in the winter through the ice on the Lena River. We dried enough meat to make it through the winters. We had our reindeer herds and milk. During the dust storms we stayed inside our yurts until the storm stopped. When the weather was good in summer, we gathered berries and herbs.

"We noticed that the fresh water from the Lena River froze more easily than the salty water of Lake Arctica. The river Lena would freeze while the salty lake stayed ice-free. One summer, the flooding from the melting ice caps in the mountains was especially severe. We watched the fresh, dirty water fan out over the salty lake. Then late that summer, ice formed early where the water of the Lena River flows over Lake Arctica. Then we realized that the fresh water floated on the salt water. This helped the ice to grow on Lake Arctica.

"Then the next fall and winter it became colder than we could ever remember. Storm after storm came. Our sun god had become too weak to fight the creeping ice monster. But this time, the sea ice spread rapidly toward the North Star as far as we could see. Lake Arctica froze over.

"We also noticed that once Lake Arctica froze, the land became even colder and drier. Keeping warm and finding enough food became harder and harder for our tribe. For the animals, Siberia became a death trap. Most of the horses, bison, and many of the big animals died or fled. There was none left, except the woolly mammoths."

"Why didn't the woolly mammoths move away when all of these changes came?" Eric asked.

"We heard that some of the woolly mammoths moved away from the North Star, but the bogs were

Fact Box

1) Bogs increased in Siberia toward the end of the Ice Age.

2) Dust storms increased late in the Ice Age.

3) The shore of the Arctic Ocean was moving south.

4) Fresh water floating on salt water will form sea ice much faster.

5) Mammoths and other animals likely became trapped on the New Siberian Islands when sea level rapidly rose.

6) There are many mammoth bone huts buried by wind-blown silt in the Ukraine and a few other countries.

Fact Box

worse away from Lake Arctica. We also know that some drowned in the rivers. So, they congregated close to the lake before Lake Arctica froze. After the lake froze, the woolly mammoths began dying out rapidly."

WOOLLY MAMMOTHS TRAPPED ON THE NEW SIBERIAN ISLANDS

Tungus raised his hand, motioning for a chance to speak. "Father, can I tell them about the woolly mammoths that became trapped on the New Siberian Hills?"

Yakut nodded approval.

Tungus began, "Lake Arctica had been slowly rising and spreading away from the North Star for many moons, as my father said. Then one summer day, Lake Arctica rose very fast. Fortunately, we were settled on a hill at the time. We watched as the woolly mammoths and other animals that lived by the coast stampeded toward the New Siberian Hills. But soon Lake Arctica surrounded the hills. There was only a little grass on the islands but a great many woolly mammoths and a few other animals. We did not think they could live there very long. I imagine the poor beasts starved to death. There were so many woolly mammoths trapped on one of those islands that we called it Bone Island. Shortly after that we moved away from the Lake. We now call those hills the New Siberian Islands."

THE LAND OF THE RISING SUN

Gath had a question that had puzzled him for a long time. Looking at Yakut, he asked, "Many moons ago another tribe from Siberia passed by our caves. They mentioned a distant land toward the rising sun from Siberia they called Alaska. They said that there was another huge land beyond there. Do you know anything about this land?"

Yakut remembered, "Our ancestors told us that many tribes had passed through Siberia. They traveled toward the rising sun following the herds of mammoths. One day a small group returned. They told us about the new land and their adventures. As I recall they named the land Alaska. They told us about a very long wide path beyond Alaska. Both sides of the path had walls of ice. Mountain peaks could be seen in the distance toward the setting sun. Many lakes dotted the ice-free path. Large herds of animals followed the path to a new land away from the North Star. The wind in the path was so miserable that men and animals traveled through it as quickly as they could, dodging the lakes. But, we heard at the end of this wide path was a vast country filled with giant herds of bison, mammoths, horses, camels, and other animals. The hunting was better there than in any of the lands they had ever traveled.

"I remember asking the men, 'Why didn't you stay in that wonderful land?' Their faces became saddened. They told us that they liked to travel. Their ancestors had spent many, many moons in that land. One day they decided to travel back toward the North Star through the ice-free path and into Alaska. On the way to Alaska, they noticed that the path was narrower than their ancestors told them. They hunted in Alaska for many moons. Then the weather and land changed in Alaska just like it did in Siberia. They tried to go back to the wide land away from the North Star. The ice had covered up the path, and they were trapped in Alaska. That is why they were migrating toward the setting sun, away from Alaska. They crossed into Siberia just before a large flood covered the low area that connected Lake Arctica with Lake Pacifica. They could no longer go back to Alaska. They continued traveling toward the setting sun for several moons until they arrived at the Lena River."

"Maybe the woolly mammoths could still be found in that land beyond the once ice-free path?" asked Eric.

WOOLLY MAMMOTH BURIED IN BLOWING DUST

Jabeth asked Yakut, "Did you leave Siberia when Lake Arctica froze? Whatever happened to the woolly mammoths? Did the animals die of the cold and bogs? Did they starve to death?"

Yakut answered, "At first we were determined to stay. This was our home and there were still enough woolly mammoths to hunt and food to gather — until one terrible winter. It was the coldest winter we could remember. When we breathed, ice crystals fell at our feet. The air was so cold. We had to cover our mouths with fur so we could breathe. The dust storms lasted longer, sometimes up to a week.

"Finally, our food was running low. It was difficult hunting because of the dust storms. We were becoming desperate. One day after a dust storm ended, we ventured out to hunt. We were a long way from home when we saw a dark rolling cloud on the horizon. It quickly grew larger

Yakut thought a bit and began, "In the land at the end of the ice-free path, grass grew over the heads of many of the animals. Hunting was so good that most of the tribes thought it would never end.

"But, then we heard from another tribe passing through our area. The climate and land was changing there too, just like in Siberia and Alaska. Huge dust storms blew. Animals were being trapped in bogs and sinkholes. In the late summer, some of these sinkholes contained the only water for miles. The tribe remembered many dead mammoths in one sinkhole in particular."

and we knew it would soon fill the sky. We were terrified. We knew we could not make it back to our homes before the storm hit. We had to find shelter as soon as possible. We dashed to a nearby rock outcrop and hid behind it. We covered our heads with furs so we could breathe. We huddled close to each other. The winds tore at our clothes and blew our provisions away. Several times we nearly panicked. I reminded the men that storms eventually end. This one seemed to last forever, but finally the winds stopped. We were cold and hungry and glad we were still alive.

"We crawled out from under our furs and discovered that deep mounds of dirt had settled on the other side of our shelter. We noticed that many skeletons of dead animals that we saw earlier were buried in the dust. It was as if they were swallowed by the earth. We knew that the bones and tusks of the woolly mammoth would soon be frozen in the ground.

"On our way home, we saw many animals were not as lucky as we were. They had died in the storm and were partly covered with dirt. Then we saw a strange sight. A woolly mammoth was mostly buried in dust. At first we thought it

was alive but when we looked closer we saw it must have suffocated sometime during the storm. The poor beast had put its back to the wind to wait out the storm but by the time the storm was over the dirt had settled above its legs. Strangely, it was still standing in the mound. As we dug it out, we saw that one of its legs was broken. The beast must have tried to pull itself out of the packed dirt and broke its leg. Cold from the ground had already crept up into the dust. The cold air and the cold from the frozen soil below were freezing the woolly mammoth as it stood.

"The sight of the buried woolly mammoth made us realize that we could have died in the dust storm. We could have been buried like the woolly mammoth. We realized that even the mighty woolly mammoth was not safe in Siberia. We decided that it was time to follow the mighty Lena to find a new home.

"You asked about the woolly mammoths. It is true that a few were dying of the cold. Most of them are so hairy that they could stand the cold. A few were dying of a lack of grass. Some were trapped in bogs. We think that most of the woolly mammoths were killed and buried in dust storms.

We saw very few woolly mammoths as we escaped up the Lena River to Lake Baikal. We believe the woolly mammoths have probably died out completely in Siberia by now."

The Westward Journey

The fire was burning low and the night was late, but no one wanted to sleep yet. They wanted to hear more. Eric asked Yakut, "We heard about your journey from Lake Arctica up the Lena River to Lake Baikal. Why did you leave Lake Baikal and travel so far to our little valley?"

"The trip from Siberia to Lake Baikal took only two moons. We hoped to make our home at Lake Baikal, but it did not take us long to discover the people were not friendly. One night a hunting party stole some of our women. We had to give them ivory to buy the women back. When they were captives, the women learned how to make jewelry out of amber and shells, so it wasn't all bad. We stayed near Lake Baikal only one summer. A terrible disease broke out among the Baikal tribes' people. Entire villages were wiped out. We left before it came to our yurts. We were sad to leave the beautiful Lake Baikal. We decided to try to find our Siberian friends we heard had moved on to the Shining Mountains.

"Since we still had our sleds, dogs, and reindeer, we left with the first snow. We traveled toward the setting sun. We moved fast on our sleds across the rolling hills. We crossed many frozen rivers. The land was a mixture of open prairie and trees. We hunted a strange deer or elk that we had never seen before. The animals had large, heavy antlers.

"We met a few friendly tribes that had seen our friends traveling through the area several summers before. We traded mammoth ivory for hides and food. The tribes used the ivory to carve animals, birds, mammoths, and snakes. They would sometimes color them with red ochre. They loved to carve female figurines for their local gods. They told us that the country between the forest and the Shining Mountains was good land. There was plenty of open space and animals to hunt and rivers to fish. Winters were not too cold and summers were actually becoming hot. They also warned us about the dust storms that made living there miserable.

"We heard that the Shining Mountains were still farther toward the setting sun. Finally, in the distance we could see the Shining Mountains rising

buried a hut, so that the people had to dig out the bones and rebuild it. Sometimes the dust covered the hut so deeply that the people abandoned it. The people who lived there told us that many huts are buried in the ground. Even there the yurts in the small villages were made of mammoth bones and tusks.

"What were the people like?" interjected Eric.

"Most of them were friendly. They prized shells and decorated their clothes with them. Many of the shells they found were in the rocks. The people carved ivory. They especially made birds and female figurines.

"We still hoped to find a home that did not have terrible dust storms. So, after we rested and refreshed our supplies, we headed toward the setting sun. The snow was melting and the rivers were high. We swam across most rivers, but sometimes we found floating logs to help us cross. Finally we came to your river, which was not flooding and was peaceful. We decided to head toward the North Star along the river. That is how we came to your valley."

out of the prairie. We searched for our friends from Siberia for one moon. The Shining Mountains was not a good place for us to settle. It was too dry. We were not able to find our friends. So, we continued our journey toward the setting sun.

"We traveled away from the Shining Mountains and dropped onto a wide open plain. It took a moon to travel across it. We heard they had terrible dust storms in that land during the spring. The snow kept the dust from blowing in winter. We still had to be careful of blizzards.

"Then, one day some snowy mountains loomed before us. The tribes in the area called them the Ural Mountains and told us of a passage around the mountains away from the North Star. We followed this route and continued on a low flat plain for several more moons. By spring, we were toward the North Star from a lake called the Black Lake. The tribes there had yurts made of mammoth bones and skins."

"What was the land of the mammoth huts like?" Eric asked.

Tungus continued the story, "By the time we arrived, the snow was melting. The dust storms were strong there too. They sometimes partially

Chapter Six

A New Life for the Siberian Tribe

It was quite late at night. Jabeth dismissed the gathering in the longhouse. He and Eric walked back to their hut.

Eric asked his father, "Where will these people go? They seem very nice. Can they stay with us?"

Jabeth smiled at his enthusiasm and said, "We will see if they want to stay."

The Long Journey Has Ended

The next morning dawned bright and sunny. After breakfast, the elders gathered back in the lodge. Jabeth motioned for all the women and children to leave. Eric was disappointed he could not stay. He asked, "Please, Father, can I listen?" Jabeth remembered when he was young and wanted so much to be included. "Yes, you may. It is about time you learn the way of the elders," said Jabeth.

Jabeth discussed accepting Yakut and his clan into their village with the tribal leaders. Later he invited Yakut, Tungus, and the other men from the Siberian tribe into the lodge.

Jabeth began, "We see that your tribe has undergone many hardships. You appear to be hard-working, brave, and honest. If you would like to make your home with us, you are welcome to stay. There is room for both tribes in this valley. We can use the help. Nabor and his thieves are growing in numbers. There is a good spot just down the river from us. We will help you build huts. You can use our longhouse for protection."

Eric was excited; he was hoping that he would be able to keep his new friend. Yakut looked to the men of his tribe. They nodded their approval. Yakut spoke, "We are very grateful for your invitation. This is a pleasant valley. The river has many fish. The hunting is not as good as where we came from, but there are enough animals for all of us. We would like to learn how to grow a garden. Our tribe is few. Together we will be stronger and more able to fight those who want to destroy the peace of this valley."

Yakut thanked Eric and his family for the rescue and for the food and gave them gifts of shells. Jabeth accepted them with gratitude. He knew Yakut had very few possessions. He did not want to insult him by refusing his generosity. The rest of the day was spent with Jabeth and Yakut, with the help of Gath, planning the new group of huts.

The next morning all of the men met. They gathered downriver and cleared the land. Poles were gathered from the forests and set into foundation stones. More poles were used to frame the roof. The women and children went out to gather straw and wove them into large mats. The walls were made out of wood and clay. After they dried, the straw mats were layered over the roof frame and tightly secured. The mats worked well. Rain and snow slid easily off of their new roofs and kept everyone dry. Next, they cleared the land to plant winter vegetables.

The Tribes Work Together

Eric worked hard that summer teaching Tungus and his family how to grow vegetables in a garden. Jabeth taught Yakut how to make metal tools. All the while they became better and better at understanding each other. Eric and Tungus always managed to find time to slip away to throw stones in the river. They often fished the river together. Eric and Tungus explored the hills surrounding the valleys. They learned new ways to hunt and fish from each other.

One day Eric saw Kolyma watching his older sister, Nama. She giggled and blushed. By the time they harvested the garden in late summer, he saw his older sister and Kolyma holding hands. "Yuck," he said to Tungus, "they like each other and will probably even kiss. Girls! I hope to never kiss one. I would rather hunt and fish."

Tungus looked a little puzzled at Eric and began to laugh, "Girls are cute and I want to kiss one someday. Hey, it happens to everybody." He shrugged and smiled in response to Eric's disgusted look. "I am thirteen and you're only twelve. You will change your mind soon, trust me."

THE SIBERIAN PEOPLE ACCEPT THE CREATOR GOD

One summer day, Yakut came up to Jabeth and asked to address all the people in the longhouse. That evening as the sun was setting, Jabeth gathered all the men and some of the women and children that would fit into the longhouse. They were now able to communicate with each other without Gath. Eric noticed that Kolyma and Nama were sitting next to each other.

Yakut rose to speak. "We have finished a long journey. We are finished wandering over the face of the earth. This is a prosperous valley. You are a good people. My wife, Ama, was talking with Ania, wondering why your tribe should help a strange people from a strange land. Ania said that it was because God is good. The Creator God blessed and protected you and wants you to help strangers. We thought our gods would help us, but many times they failed."

Yakut continued, "Gath told me that our gods were just images from the mind, but there is the one true God. He made the earth, the sun, the moon and the stars, fire, and wind. By your teaching and by our own eyes we can see that He has provided everything for us that we need to live. He has made the beauty that makes our hearts sing. He has given us good friends. We know the

Creator God made the people who rebelled against Him. Now we understand why there was a Flood. He had the right to destroy us when we rebelled against Him. It all makes sense to us. We have decided that we do not want to forget the Creator God who saved our ancestors and us. We will destroy our ivory gods and our amulets because they do not honor the Creator of all things." Jabeth, Eric, and all of the tribe cheered. There was great happiness knowing that they were of one mind and heart loving and serving the Creator.

Fact Box

1) The use of metal tools likely developed rapidly after leaving the caves.

2) People who lived during the Ice Age were smart and could learn to adapt to their new surroundings.

3) From tribal groups in huts, towns and cities soon flourished after the Ice Age.

4) Agriculture, the use of metal tools, and civilization started rapidly at the end of the Ice Age.

Fact Box

Part II

Chapter Seven

The End of the Great Ice Age

The Ice Age — Still A Major Mystery of Science

After 160 years, evolutionists have yet to find a cause for the Ice Age that does not have fatal flaws. We are convinced that this is because they hold tenaciously to the evolutionist axiom, "the present is the key to the past." One present process they use is very slight changes in the power of the sun that takes place in the high latitudes over time. These changes are caused by slight changes in the earth's orbit around the sun. Scientists have worked these factors backwards and think they have a good theory for an ice age. Since these factors repeat over time, they have come to accept there were many ice ages that cycled every 100,000 years. This is called the astronomical theory of the ice ages.

The problem with their theory is the changes in the earth's orbit are too small to cause the radical temperature drop needed for an ice age. The summers have to be much colder than they are today. They have to be so cold that the winter snow does not melt, and they have to experience frequent heavy snowstorms. Computer rendering indicates the summer temperatures in northeast Canada would have to fall more than 20 degrees Fahrenheit for the winter snow to remain through the summer. Along the southern edge of the ice sheets, the problem is much worse. Minneapolis, Minnesota, was covered by ice at the edge of the ice sheet in the fairly recent past. For Minneapolis to develop an ice sheet, the summer temperatures would have to drop from the current average of 70 degrees Fahrenheit to well below 32 degrees Fahrenheit. The average would likely be about 20 degrees Fahrenheit or below. This is a cooling of fifty degrees! Adding to the challenge is that every summer would have to be this cold for hundreds of years! Present processes do not hold the key to this mystery.

Adding to the puzzle, we know that during the Ice Age the spring, summer, and autumn were colder than today. We also know that the colder the air, the less moisture it holds. So, where did the vast quantities of snow come from?

These many apparently unsolvable problems are why there are over 60 hypotheses on the cause of the Ice Age besides the currently popular astronomical hypothesis. This is why *U. S. News and World Report*

One of the most distinctive lateral and terminal moraines in the world is in the northern Wallowa Mountains in northeast Oregon.

Ground level view of the 700-foot-high (210 m) lateral moraine.

said in 1997 that the cause of the Ice Age is one of 18 major mysteries of science (Watson, 1997). David Alt (2001) stated in a recent book on the Lake Missoula flood: "Although theories abound, no one really knows what causes Ice Ages."

TELLTALE SIGNS OF PAST ICE SHEETS

If an ice age is this difficult to develop, how do we know there was an Ice Age? We know there was an Ice Age when we examine glaciers today. Modern glaciers leave behind certain telltale signs. These same features are seen over large parts of the world where there are no glaciers today.

Glacial till is found in many places where the ice has been. Till is composed of rocks of many sizes surrounded by clay, silt, or sand. Sometimes the till forms linear mounds called moraines. Moraines form when ice pushes rocks and dirt to the edge of the glaciers as it moves. Moraines in the front of a glacier are called terminal or end moraines. Moraines at the side of a glacier are called lateral moraines. The movement of the rocks and ice below an ice sheet causes scratches or grooves in the bedrock. The rocks in the ice at the bottom (foot) of a glacier also become scratched.

When we examine the regions where till and other glacial features are found, we discover that the ice sheets once covered much of northern Europe, northwest Asia, and northern North America. Ice caps even covered up many mountainous areas of the world. The scratches on the rocks have not been erased and the moraines are often sharply crested. The fact that erosion has not destroyed delicate features is evidence that the Ice Age ended recently.

Interestingly, we learned that ice caps developed in the mountains of Siberia, Alaska, and the Yukon Territory. Yet, the lowlands of these regions were never glaciated. This is very puzzling to evolutionary scientists. When scientists run computer programs on glaciation, Alaska and Siberia sometimes are the first to glaciate. This ice develops both in the mountains and lowlands in these programs. The reason these lowlands were never glaciated is because the Ice Age was much different than evolutionary scientists believe.

Moraine (with musk ox in foreground)

43

The Genesis Flood Caused the Ice Age

The worldwide flood of Noah's time is the best explanation for what caused the Ice Age (Oard, 1990; 2004b). This was explained in chapter 7 of *Life in the Great Ice Age* (Oard and Oard, 1993).

The Flood was a giant volcanic event with much earth movement. After the Flood, a huge amount of dust and gases would have been left in the upper atmosphere. The dust and gases would have

Leaving the Caves

• The story of Jabeth, Eric, and their family took place as the Great Ice Age ended. The climate toward the end of the Ice Age is briefly described in *Life in the Great Ice Age*. The pressures of the climate, wild animals, and the environment forced people to use caves as a refuge. Caves did not require building. They were strong and provided some protection from animals and the elements. Rocks were handy tools to use, since caves are made of them. They used all of the resources available to them to survive the cold and the dangers of wild animals.

• This book describes the shift from caves to villages. The climate changes accelerated in Eric's generation as the Ice Age ended. The difference between summer and winter widened; summers continued to become warmer and winters colder. The woolly mammoth, Irish elk, woolly rhinoceros, and saber-toothed tiger went extinct. The warmer summers and increasing human population motivated many people to move out of their caves and into huts. They formed small villages. This was a time of transition. Archaeology shows hunting and gathering were still practiced, but agriculture and herding of tame animals developed quickly near and within formerly glaciated areas. Goats and reindeer were among some of the animals they successfully tamed. They hunted wild boar, deer, elk, and small game, instead of woolly mammoths. Most big game of the Ice Age slowly disappeared. Tribes often traded seeds and ideas with one another.

reflected much sunlight back to space. This reflected sunlight would not have been able to heat the ground. As observed after the eruption of modern volcanoes, the dust and gases fall to the ground over several years. Dust and gases would have been replenished in the upper atmosphere from a great amount of volcanoes going off during the Ice Age (Oard, 1990). Such volcanism would have lasted for several hundred years after the Flood.

The Ice Age would have needed very heavy precipitation. The Flood would have added hot water from the Fountains of the Great Deep and lava flows to the oceans. After the Flood, the ocean would have been much warmer, probably around 86°F (30°C) on average. The warmer the water, the more it evaporates into the atmosphere. This evaporation would have mostly occurred at mid and high latitudes, close to the rapidly developing ice sheets. Based on the cooling time of the oceans, the Ice Age would have lasted about 700 years.

The Flood answers most or all of the problems that evolutionary scientists struggle with. There was really only one Ice Age. Best of all, we really do not need to fear a future Ice Age because of the sign of the rainbow. If there will never be another global flood, there also will never be another ice age.

Leaving the Caves

The building of villages started rapidly after people left the caves of northern Europe, not slowly as has been assumed by archeologists. Many ancient villages were built close to rivers. Rivers provided water, fish, travel, and trade. In fact, anthropologists now realize that many of their ideas about the origin of agriculture may be wrong. Creationists believe anthropologists' major problem is their long time scale. There are some archeologists who now believe agriculture could have developed rapidly in Europe:

The realization that recent hunter-gatherers can turn to herding and crop cultivation if they perceive this to be advantageous has major implications for studies of agricultural origins in Europe (Dennell, 1992).

The people leaving the caves needed only to experiment and use the materials provided for them. These men were as smart as modern people. Rapid travel and trade would have provided the seeds and shared knowledge necessary for the spread of agriculture in Europe. For thousands of years farmers used the slash and burn method of preparing the ground for new crops.

Archaeologists and anthropologists have divided up the time before active city building into four main periods or ages based on the materials used for tools. These are the Paleolithic age (old stone age), Neolithic age (new stone age), the Bronze age, and the Iron age. These divisions developed in the 1800s and assumed evolution. In spite of their belief, many archaeologists have come to realize that this classification scheme is an oversimplification. Chris Scarre (1998) writes:

We saw earlier how the nineteenth-century scheme for European prehistory divides it into a sequence of ages based on the material used for cutting tools — first stone, then bronze, then iron. Archaeologists today realize that while these can be useful divisions, they don't necessarily correspond to major changes in the way prehistoric people lived or prehistoric communities functioned.

The assumption of evolution forces the archaeologist to fit what he finds into his framework. Evolution requires millions of years, and assumes man evolved from an ape or ape-like ancestor. Accordingly, it took an exceedingly long time for them to learn to speak, use tools, and develop civilization. The evolutionists also assume that tools evolved as people became smarter with time.

Creationists assume the Bible is true. We accept that God made man in His own image and likeness. In the Garden of Eden, man had a high degree of intelligence even if he didn't use it wisely. He was able to name all of the animals in the Garden in one day and to find a way to survive outside of the Garden after man sinned. As a result, he would also have been able to use his creative resources for survival during the Ice Age and for the development of agriculture and cities at the end of the Ice Age. Discovery, as well as trial and error, brought progress. However, war and disease often caused developments to be lost, if they were not shared or found useful.

There were always pockets of people in the warmer climates that had tame animals and grew limited amounts of lentils or barley. Some of this knowledge spread north as the summers warmed at the end of the Ice Age. Fishing was practiced when people lived in caves as evidenced in the caves of southern France. For those living near rivers or the ocean, fishing became a way of life after they left the caves. Archaeology has revealed abundant fishing implements and fish bones in caves as well as villages that were built close to water. When smelting ore was rediscovered, metal tools slowly replaced stone tools. Finding the ore and smelting took time. It took more time for this discovery to spread. A metal tool was highly prized and kept for generations. Creative and observant individuals, like Jabeth, made the discoveries that led the way to a better way of living. Over time, the trading of wares and ideas became more extensive. Pottery, seeds for agriculture, amber and shells, and domestic animals became items of trade beginning in southern Europe and spreading north.

THE CHANGING CLIMATE OF SIBERIA

The oral history of Tungus' tribe began after

People extracted metal from its ore by a process involving heating and melting, thus allowing the making of metal tools

People discovered new methods of farming, agriculture, agronomy, cultivation, and animal husbandry

the Flood and the Tower of Babel rebellion. Both tribes headed generally north from the "two rivers area" — the Tigris-Euphrates Valley. Eric's ancestors followed the animals as they spread into central Germany. Tungus' ancestors wandered into north-central Siberia. These migrations were inferred in the Bible as the descendents of Noah's sons spread north and east.

When Tungus' ancestors first lived on the shores of the Arctic Ocean (Lake Arctica), the winter temperatures were mild and the summers were cool. In our story they lived near the mouth of the Lena River in north-central Siberia. The Siberian tribe did not live in caves but on the flat lands of northern Siberia. They used stone tools. Their homes are called yurts in our story. The Siberians tamed reindeer and dogs. They made warm clothing of animal skins and fur.

For a few hundred years after the Flood and during the Ice Age, similar climatic and environmental conditions existed over the entire Northern Hemisphere. This included Siberia. Such a climate with cool summers and mild winters explains the mix of cold climate plants and animals with those that preferred warm climates. Reindeer and woolly mammoths lived with badgers, ferrets, antelope, and other animals that prefer warmer climates. The most interesting example of this climatic mix of animals is hippopotamuses that lived with woolly mammoths and reindeer in southern England. This was described in chapter 6 of *Life in the Great Ice Age*. Evolutionary scientists are perplexed by such a mixture, although they have a few hypotheses as to how this could be.

The mild winter climate that characterized the early Ice Age was caused by unique conditions. The Arctic Ocean and the North Pacific Ocean would be fairly warm immediately after the Flood. Cooler air from the continents would cause moisture to rise from the ocean. This was why Tungus' ancestors saw mists rise from the Arctic Ocean.

As the ice sheets grew in portions of northern North America and northern Europe, the winters in the Northern Hemisphere became colder. The oceans cooled at the same time, resulting in less evaporation. The colder winters brought less snowfall. Grasslands replaced most of the forests, including Siberia. It is on these grasslands that the woolly mammoths, woolly rhinoceroses, bison, horses, and many other animals thrived.

At the end of the Ice Age, the summers became warmer, so the ice sheets in the mountains began to melt. The rivers swelled. Many areas were flooded, and vast amounts of fresh water poured over the Arctic Ocean. It was during this time that the ocean froze. In our story, Tungus' ancestors and family experienced many of these changes.

Tungus' ancestors first noted that the shoreline of Lake Arctica moved north. This was because the sea level dropped as the water evaporated and snow was deposited on land during the Ice Age. The continental shelf off northern Siberia is very shallow. The falling sea level would move the shoreline hundreds of miles north. The New Siberian Islands to the northeast of the Lena River delta would become part of the coast. It was not until the melting stage of the Ice Age that they became islands once again. This is why the islands were called the New Siberian Hills in our story, until the rapid rise in sea level.

Tungus' tribe lived a few hundred years in northern Siberia until they were forced to flee. Their food became scarce as the large mammals died. The dust storms intensified. They traveled to Lake Baikal in southern Siberia in the hope of a better life. Later, they migrated westward toward the Shining Mountains, which are the Tien Shan Mountains, and on to central Germany. There they are rescued from a thieving tribe by Eric's tribe. Eric's tribe knew the real Creator God and showed hospitality to the strange tribe from Siberia. The two tribes got to know each other. It did not take long for Tungus' tribe to decide to join Eric's tribe. The tribes would form a larger village and intermarry.

The people built a tower in an attempt to reach heaven (Gen. 11:1–9).

Archaeologists have little evidence that man lived in northern Siberia with the woolly mammoths during the Great Ice Age. It is possible the wind-blown dust, called loess, has covered most archaeological sites. However, archaeologists reported in 2003 the discovery of a site on the Yana River, east of the Lena River, in northern Siberia (Pitulko, et al., 2004; Stone, 2004). They were surprised to find man was able to survive the Ice Age that far north. Evolutionists envision an Ice Age that was colder than Siberia is today. The Flood-Ice Age theory predicts Ice Age winters were much warmer. It is not surprising to creation scientists that archaeological sites are found that far north. Evolutionary scientists were further surprised to find artifacts that are similar to those found in North America. These include foreshafts of spears carved from mammoth ivory and an artifact fashioned from the horn of a woolly rhinoceros. These similarities indicate that man traveled from Siberia into North America (Oard, 2004b). It is possible that some tribes may have returned to Alaska and Siberia from southern North America, as the one tribe we describe in the story.

Dust Storms While Ice Sheets Melt

The Great Ice Age was a consequence of the worldwide flood described in the Bible. Hot water from the Fountains of the Great Deep mixed with the cooler pre-flood ocean. Evaporation from the warmed oceans joined with air from the colder continents. This created powerful storms that dumped huge amounts of snow over much of the northern latitudes. In about 500 years, the oceans had cooled enough to slow and eventually stop this dynamic engine. At this time the ice began to melt. The melting picked up speed and giant floods swept the lowlands in some areas. The Lake Missoula flood is a good example of this (Oard, 2004a). At the same time, powerful winds whipped up and deposited loess over vast stretches of land. Increasing evidence is surfacing that indicates ice sheets during the Ice Age were about half the thickness scientists originally assumed (Oard, 1990). While other ice sheets melted, the Greenland and Antarctic ice sheets grew because of their high latitude and altitude.

Ice cores on these ice sheets have reached ice claimed to be hundreds of thousands of years old. However, this interpretation is based on their assumption that the ice sheets are millions of years old. There is an alternative method of interpreting the data based on the rapid post-Flood Ice Age (Oard, 2004b, 2005).

The rapid melting of the ice sheets, strangely enough, was enhanced by the colder winters. Colder winters produced much less snow. Since the snow did not build up as much, the warmer summers could do their work of melting the ice. As winters became colder, the colder air spread out over the oceans, causing the oceans to also cool at the end of the Ice Age. There is much less evaporation from a cold ocean, so the atmosphere became drier.

In *Life in the Great Ice Age*, Grandfather had predicted Jabeth would see the ice sheets completely melt. Each year they were receding. The summer heat was enough to not only melt the previous winter's light snowfall, but also about 30 feet (about 10 meters) of ice from the top of the ice sheets. During Eric's lifetime, the ice had melted off the northern continent of Europe and northwest Asia. It was also melting rapidly in Scandinavia. Between Scandinavia and continental Europe, a large body of water opened up that for a while was a lake and eventually connected with the ocean. This is now the Baltic Sea that Eric's tribe called Lake Baltica. Because the ice left northern continental Europe, Eric and his family were able to move farther north and develop a settlement along a river.

Winter and summer temperatures warmed first in the lower latitudes, near the equator. This signaled the beginning of the end of the Ice Age on the tropical mountains. When the tropics warmed, a strong temperature difference developed between the equator and the poles. The temperature difference was far greater than the one that exists today.

Loess, a loosely compacted yellowish-gray deposit of windblown sediment, occurs extensively in some areas

This caused strong west winds to blow across the middle latitudes, and possibly the higher latitudes as well. These winds were so strong that they picked up topsoil and deposited it over vast regions. In the Northern Hemisphere there are places where the loess is over 100 feet deep (about 30 m), for instance, in the lowlands of Siberia and Alaska. Interestingly, the experts on Ice Age animals in Siberia have found that most of the woolly mammoths and other animals are buried in thick layers of loess.

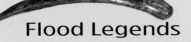

Flood Legends

• Tungus' tribe had forgotten God, but remembered the Flood and the dispersal after the Tower of Babel rebellion. They confused some of the details and added their gods into the events. There are hundreds of such flood legends from people groups all over the earth. These legends indicate a common event that people remember. Many of the details of these myths range anywhere from improbable to impossible, but multiple flood legends give further evidence that there was a worldwide flood deeply etched in mankind's memory.

• The account of the Flood in the Bible is so reasonable that it is apparent that it is the original. Other legends are variations of it. The biblical ark is built like a monstrous barge with an extremely stable length to width ratio of six to one. It would have been nearly impossible to sink. Contrast the ark dimensions with the boat in the Epic of Gilgamesh. This tale is the closest geographically (the people group lived close to the Hebrews) and in detail to the one in the Bible. Their boat is described as cube shaped, 120 feet (35 m) on each side. Such a shape is unstable in rough water. This type of boat would tend to rotate around and around. Within a few days the people and animals would be dead from the constant tumbling in rough seas.

• In our story, Eric's family had memorized the details of the Flood and the Babel dispersion and passed them from generation to generation. They were careful to not change any of it. Eric and his family told the Siberian tribe the story. Tungus and his family recognized it as the original. The love and hospitality that Jabeth extended won their hearts and eventually they dedicated their lives to the Creator God.

North and Central America

Polynesia

Traditional/Middle East

Russia/Scandinavia

China/Oriental

Chapter Eight

LIFE AND DEATH OF THE WOOLLY MAMMOTH

Our story of the woolly mammoths focuses mainly in Siberia, but their bones are also found in northern Europe, north-west Asia, and North America. The main problem for evolutionists is why so many of them congregated along the Arctic Ocean in the inhospitable north country of Siberia and how they died.

We have described the post-Flood climate changes throughout our story and in more detail earlier. In this section we will focus mainly on the woolly mammoths and other mammals at the end of the Ice Age (Oard, 2004b).

THE ELEPHANT KIND

After the Genesis flood, the animals spread over all of the earth. The woolly mammoth was among them. It is not known whether mammoths are a separate Genesis kind or not. It is more likely that the woolly mammoth, mastodons, and the modern Asian and African elephant all derive from the same elephant kind. A woolly mammoth is essentially a hairy elephant with a hump on its head and a sloping back. They have the same digestive system as modern elephants and likely a similar disposition. The woolly mammoth is sometimes portrayed as a fierce beast, but this is likely

Woolly Mammoth   *American Mastodon*   *African elephant*   *Indian elephant*

not true. With time the elephants would have diverged into different varieties after leaving the ark. Genetically, it would be much the same way that wolves, poodles, and great danes diverged within the dog kind. All of the genetic information for the varieties would have existed in the original parents on Noah's ark. After spreading from the mountains of Ararat, the varieties within the kind would have separated out by the pressures of the environment and climate.

The Columbian mammoth is similar to the woolly mammoth. It also is a variety of elephant. It generally lived south of the range of the woolly mammoth in North America, Europe, and Asia. Evolutionary scientists in Europe and Asia give the Columbian mammoth different names.

It is the biblical kind and not the manmade definition of species that is the basic reproductive unit in the Bible. The first chapter of Genesis states ten times that animals and plants are made after their own kind. They would reproduce within their kinds. The Bible is directly contrary to the idea of evolution, which claims every organism shares common ancestors. Many creationist biologists are actively involved in research to determine the Genesis kinds of different animals. This research is called baraminology. With humans we know that we are all one kind — we are all one blood as the Bible says. Adam and Eve began with all of the genetic information for all of the varieties of man that descended from the original gene pool. We can also include Neanderthal Man and *Homo erectus* in the human kind (Lubenow, 2004).

God created the gene pool perfect at the beginning. Mutations, the vast majority of which are harmful or lethal, have occurred since man sinned. At the beginning it was no problem for Cain and Seth to marry one of their sisters, since Adam and Eve had many sons and daughters (Gen. 5:4). The mutations in the gene pool have built up with time, which is why God forbade brother-sister marriages at the time of Moses.

Recognizing the Genesis kind as the basic biological unit solves many difficulties. Skeptics declare there was not enough room on the ark for all of the animals. The definition of kind is pivotal. Kinds mostly correlate with the genus or family level, not the species level. Two of each kind of animal would require far fewer animals. Genesis says that the animals that were to go into the ark were those that lived on land and breathed air. This eliminates marine creatures, among others. If the biblical kind compares to the genus level of biological classification, then Noah would have had to take only about 16,000 animals on the ark (Woodmorappe, 1996). There would have been plenty of room for the animals, including land dinosaurs. Since there were probably only about 50 kinds of dinosaurs, Noah needed only 100 dinosaurs on the ark. Many dinosaurs were the size of a chicken and have an average size of a sheep. It would make sense that God would lead juveniles, not the larger adults, onto the ark.

Woolly Mammoths Spread into Siberia Early in the Ice Age

Whether woolly mammoths are a distinct kind or a variety of the elephant kind doesn't matter much. Eventually, woolly mammoths spread from the mountains of Ararat northward into Siberia. Why would they want to live in Siberia? Siberia today is bitterly cold and dark in winter and a dangerous bog land in summer.

The first question to ask is: How many woolly mammoths are buried in the permafrost? Permafrost is made up of wedge or icicle-shaped ice, called ice wedges, and lenses of ground ice (following page). The warmer summers caused the top two feet (about 0.5 m) of frozen soil to melt. If it were only a few mammoths, it would not be significant. We would expect a few adventuresome hairy elephants to explore and become stuck in Siberia. But if it were millions, then there is a real problem explaining their existence so far north.

To find out the number, we go to scientists who have studied the woolly mammoths in Siberia. These scientists almost always describe the number of mammal remains in the permafrost as very high. The top expert on Siberian Ice Age animals for over 50 years was Nikolai Vereshchagin. He estimated that between the Kolyma and Yana Rivers in the vicinity of the New Siberian Islands, there are around five million mammoths buried in the permafrost or lying on the bottom of the shallows of the Arctic Ocean. When all of Siberia, Alaska, and the Yukon are counted together, the number would be closer to ten million in the far north. This number does not include the millions more that lived in Europe and passed through the ice-free corridor and into the United States.

Nearly all the animals that lived in Siberia were grazers that ate a wide variety of grasses. Along with the woolly mammoth are fossils of bison, horses, woolly rhinos, wolverines, moose, reindeer, musk oxen, and other animals. Cave lions also lived in Siberia and Alaska at the end of the Ice Age. This inspired the story of the cave lion attack on Tungus' grandfather and brothers. Dale Guthrie (1990) provides more evidence that lions lived in Alaska. A bison carcass, Blue Babe, found near Fairbanks, Alaska, was injured and/or killed by a lion. Scratch marks, bite marks, and even a broken tooth were found in the carcass.

The Irish elk, a giant deer, is found in southern Siberia near Lake Baikal. It is also found westward to the Atlantic Ocean. The Irish elk had huge antlers and likely was well adapted to its environment. Tungus describes hunting them when they left the Lake Baikal area while the tribe migrated toward the setting sun.

Dale Guthrie of the University of Alaska has studied the environmental implications of all these animals living in the far north. Because practically all these animals were grazers, Guthrie has called the region the mammoth steppe (pronounced step). The Ice Age mammoth steppe included the region from France east to Alaska and the Yukon. A steppe climate has fairly wet springs and is dry from late summer into winter and favors the growth of grass. Guthrie (1990) describes the mammoth steppe as rich, with fertile soil, warmer winters, early springs, and long growing seasons. These grasslands would have provided plenty of food for giant herds of large mammals. Such an environment in Siberia is very different from the environment of today.

The millions of woolly mammoth bones and other mammals discovered in the permafrost of Siberia is a problem for evolutionists. We know that the woolly mammoth population increased wherever the environment favored them. Evolutionists believe that the woolly mammoths lived in Siberia either during an interglacial or a glacial period. There are problems with either belief. If the mammoths lived during a glacial period, temperatures would be much colder than today. It is doubtful that all the mammals that lived in Siberia could thrive. There would be little to eat with colder temperatures.

Some evolutionists believe the woolly mammoths inhabited Siberia during a little warmer climate of an interglacial period (Agenbroad, and Nelson, 2002). However, the bogs would still be there in summer. This is the main problem. Today much of Siberia is permafrost. The ground is permanently frozen hundreds of feet (over 100 m) deep. Only the top foot or two (about 0.5 m) melts each summer. Meltwater and rain have little place to drain, so the water forms ponds in the flat lands. It is difficult for large animals, except the reindeer, to pass through during the summer. Much of the vegetation is bog vegetation and is toxic to most grazers (Guthrie, 1990). This is further evidence that the climate of Siberia had to be dramatically different than it is today.

The rapid post-Flood Ice Age would allow for a time when Siberia was mostly grassland. This was because the winters were much warmer than today. Permafrost was rare with few bogs. It is likely that the climate at the beginning of the Ice Age was too wet for a grassland. This is because of all the moisture from the Arctic Ocean. Trees would have grown in Siberia at first. Trees are buried in the permafrost. As the Ice Age progressed, the ice sheets and cooler ocean temperatures would have resulted in a drier climate about midway into the Ice Age. This is likely the time when huge populations of mammals spread into Siberia.

There likely was little or no permafrost until the end of the Ice Age. This is another major mystery associated with what evolutionists believe about the Ice Age. The existence of a grassland with so many grazers

Mammoth Bone Huts and Figurines

• Woolly mammoths were of particular interest to man. Mammoths were commonly drawn on cave walls from Europe east into the Ural Mountains. In our story, Tungus' tribe traded in ivory. Ivory was commonly carved into many types of objects that have been found from Europe into southern Siberia. Ivory was carved into sculptures of the mammoth itself, birds, and humans. Geometric patterns have been etched or painted on tusks. Graves of Ice Age people have been found adorned with ivory staffs, daggers, needles, bracelets, carvings, and beads. Ivory tools have been found, such as shovels, spatulas, cleavers, digging sticks, and even fishhooks. Mammoth bones have been used as anvils, tables, and even parts of a barbecue pit.

• One of the more interesting uses of mammoth bones and tusks was the making of huts (Agenbroad and Nelson, 2002). In our story, Tungus and his family rested for a while with the people of the mammoth bone huts. More than 70 mammoth bone huts have been excavated from loess. These are found mainly in the Ukraine, but some can be found in the Czech Republic and Poland. The builders used the geometric shape of the bones and tusks in construction. For instance, mammoth skulls were placed in a semicircle. Jawbones were placed on top of the skulls and the walls were made of the long bones. The roof was composed of the tusks. Animal skins likely covered the mammoth bone framework. Some of these mammoth bone huts were 13 to 22 feet across and could hold 30 people. Fireplaces were also found in some of them. One site at Mezhirich, Ukraine, is composed of 150 mammoths. The weight of the dwelling can be substantial. One bone hut at Mezhirich had a total weight of 46,300 pounds (21,000 kg).

is evidence for a lack of permafrost. Many saiga antelope fossils are found in Siberia, Alaska, and the Yukon Territory. The saiga antelope has small hooves. They need a firm substrate to walk on. Fossils of badgers, ferrets, and beavers in Siberia provide further evidence for these much warmer conditions during the Ice Age because animals that burrow deep avoid permafrost. The relatively warm winters of the post-Flood rapid Ice Age would prevent permafrost from developing. Warmer winters and no permafrost are predicted by the post-Flood rapid Ice Age but are contrary to the evolutionary Ice Age hypothesis.

It is fair to ask if there was enough time after the Flood for the population of woolly mammoths to become so large. Assuming the population began with two mammoths or elephants leaving the ark, they would have increased slowly — at first. Then from geometric progression, the population would explode after about a hundred years. The population increase can be estimated from the increase in African elephants today. The doubling time for elephants on two preserves in Africa ranged from 10 to 25 years. Based on the fastest growth, the number of mammoths would be several billion in only 300 years! One would expect the faster growth rate to apply early in the Ice Age because the mammoths were spreading into mostly unoccupied territory. Other than man who hunted them during the Ice Age, mammoths had few predators. The post-Flood Ice Age lasted about 700 years (Oard, 1990). So, there would have been plenty of time for the population of woolly mammoths to grow into the millions in Siberia during the rapid Ice Age. Only man and a lack of forage and water would cut their numbers. As we have shown, forage was no problem until later in the Ice Age.

As ice accumulated on the lands of the world, the sea level fell, exposing many miles of continental shelves. The especially flat shelves north of Siberia and between Siberia and Alaska connected, forming the Bering Land Bridge. Man, along with many kinds of animals, including the bison and woolly mammoth, found a way to migrate into North America.

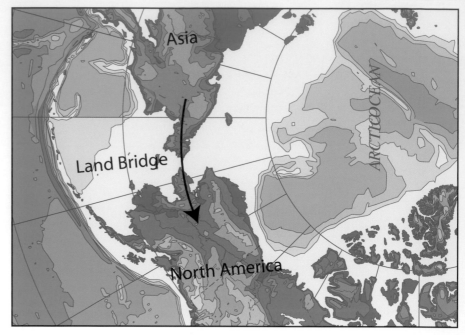

Migration route

EXTINCTION OF THE WOOLLY MAMMOTH — A MAJOR MYSTERY OF SCIENCE

Why did all of the large mammals in Siberia, except for the reindeer, disappear from Siberia by the end of the Ice Age? (Musk oxen also died out in Siberia, but have been reintroduced by man during modern times.) Many of these mammals actually became extinct over the entire world or from entire continents. The evolutionary scientists believe the end of the Ice Age was a time of warming with more land available as the ice melted. It is this assumption that leaves them scratching their heads. Why did this mass extinction occur when the climate and environment were supposed to have improved?

For the last two hundred years the mass extinction in Siberia and other lands has been a major mystery evolutionary theorists have not been able to solve. Those who cling to uniformitarianism explain the problem this way: "This great extinction — truly a mass extinction — represents one of paleontology's most fundamental mysteries" (Ward, 1997). Paleontology is the study of fossils. Agenbroad and Nelson (2002) lament: "Why did mammoths disappear from Earth? This question remains one of the great unsolved mysteries of all time."

CARCASS PUZZLES

A number of carcasses of frozen woolly mammoths, woolly rhinos, horses, and bisons have been discovered in the permafrost. When we examine these carcasses, the mystery of the disappearance of the woolly mammoths deepens. The more the scientists learn, the more it challenges their assumptions. Some unusual ideas have been suggested to answer the questions that arise.

Why are the animals so well preserved? Some of the mammals have half-decayed vegetation in their stomachs. Why didn't the flesh rot and the vegetation in the stomach completely decay? Doesn't this indicate fairly recent burial? How did it get cold enough fast enough to freeze them before they rotted? Some suggest the animals must have been frozen rapidly at temperatures colder than -150°F (-100°C). This is called the quick freeze hypothesis and was developed in the early 1800s by prominent scientists of the day. One carcass, the Berezovka mammoth, had buttercups and other plants between its clenched teeth (Pfizenmayer, 1939). Their last meal can be identified. The meal is only partially consistent with the vegetation that exists there today. Why?

A number of Siberian explorers have noted that some carcasses as well as skeletons of some animals are buried in a general standing position. Why and how did this happen? Tolmachoff (1929) states the situation:

> Brandt was very much impressed by the fact that remnants of the mammoth, carcasses and skeletons alike, sometimes were found in poses which indicated that the animals had perished standing upright, as though they had bogged.

Brandt was a Siberian explorer in the 1800s. Upright burial could indicate that the animal sunk in a bog. However, the type of sediment surrounding these carcasses is rarely bog sediment. So, we need some explanation other than sinking in a bog.

Making the problem even more complicated for the evolutionist, scientists were surprised to learn in examining the condition of the blood that three woolly mammoths and two woolly rhinos died by suffocation.

BEREZOVKA MAMMOTH

• Some of the carcasses have broken bones. The Berezovka mammoth had a broken front foreleg, a broken pelvis, and broken ribs (Pfizenmayer, 1939). The reader will note that this mammoth is in a general standing position. Although the animal slumped down a riverbank, it probably was buried in this position, since slump masses can maintain their coherency while sliding.

Another mystery associated with the carcasses is that the carcasses as well as the bones are buried in the permafrost. The permafrost is rock-hard soil and ice below the summer melt layer. How can a hairy elephant be jammed into the permafrost and remain whole before it rotted? Henry Howorth (1887) described this problem long ago:

> Now, by no physical process known to us can we understand how soft flesh could thus be buried in ground while it is frozen as hard as flint without disintegrating it. We cannot

push an elephant's body into a mass of solid ice or hard frozen gravel and clay without entirely destroying the fine articulations and pounding the whole mass into a jelly, nor would we fail in greatly disturbing the ground in the process.

There have been many attempts to explain the carcass puzzles. Some scientists have suggested rapid shifting of the pole or the earth's crust. In this way the mammoths were peacefully grazing on grass and buttercups in a mild climate and suddenly were thrown into the polar latitudes, where they froze almost instantaneously by a quick freeze. Henry Howorth proposed a shallow flood sweeping the land.

DEATH OF THE WOOLLY MAMMOTH IN SIBERIA

The post-Flood Ice Age provides viable solutions to the many questions left unanswered by those who struggle to interpret the world through uniformitarianism.

The woolly mammoths found the Siberian environment favorable early or midway through the Ice Age. Their numbers mushroomed, but the climate changed. For the last two hundred years of the Ice Age, the Siberian winters became even colder than they are today. The air became very dry. The cold, dry air greatly stressed the animals. Many of them left Siberia. The woolly mammoths were able to stand a fair amount of cold, so by the time the climate became intolerable for them, the permafrost was well developed. This caused bogs to form. Bogs took over more and more of the land at the end of the Ice Age. The mammoth steppe grassland was gradually replaced with bog vegetation that was toxic to many animals. The large feet and stiff legs of the woolly mammoth would have made navigating the tundra nearly impossible. Those animals that had not already left were trapped. The cold became nearly intolerable.

Sometimes fierce windstorms and blowing dust covered the land. As long as the Arctic Ocean remained ice-free, northern Siberia still had a fairly mild winter. This is probably why there are so many woolly mammoth remains near the Arctic Ocean. But as the ice caps melted in the mountains of Siberia and Alaska, fresh water from flooded rivers spread over the Arctic Ocean. Fresh water would

tend to float on the denser salt water. It is much easier to freeze fresh water than salt water. Each autumn, starting with the mouths of the rivers, ice gradually crept over the Arctic Ocean. Finally, enough fresh water spread over the Arctic Ocean that the entire surface of the Arctic Ocean froze over. This probably took only a few years.

When the Arctic Ocean was covered with sea ice, the air turned much colder. This made late summer and early autumn cold fronts especially vicious. One can imagine that after a warm late summer, a particularly cold storm blew into Siberia. The passage of the cold front would be a likely time for the Berezovka mammoth to die and freeze. Our story has Tungus' tribe witnessing such an event.

The question left for us is: How did they die and how are the carcass puzzles explained? There have been several ideas. The most important clue for understanding the mystery of their death is the type of sediment surrounding the bones and carcasses. When archaeologists examined material encasing the carcasses, they first thought the woolly mammoth and other animals were buried in river sediments. They also thought many of the animals died in the bogs. This could explain the standing position and suffocation of some of the animals. More evidence has since come to light. It seems that only a small number of woolly mammoths died in flooded rivers and bogs. The majority of them are buried in wind-blown silt. This silt with animal bones is now preserved as hills. The local people call the hills edomas or yedomas. Vereshchagin and Tomirdiaro (1999, p. 190-191) proclaim:

> Of particular interest for paleozoologists is the "edoma"...This is actually a loess layer, as a rule containing the largest amount of remains of Late Pleistocene animals.

One problem is the origin of so much loess in Siberia. Silt can form by glacial grinding, so that rivers coming from the glaciated mountains would spread the silt along the river floodplain. The winds would pick this up and deposit most of it downwind. However, there would not be enough of this material to cover millions of woolly mammoths. Another source for silt could be the exposed continental shelves and from mud flats that were left after the Genesis flood.

Buried in Dust Storms!

• Wind-blown silt covers much of the lowlands of Siberia. The only logical conclusion is that many woolly mammoths and other animals died and were buried in dust storms! Most of the animals likely died of the cold or drought. They decayed before finally being buried in the permafrost. Minor dust storms gradually covered up the bones and tusks. Otherwise they would rot and not be well preserved. We have Tungus and his family witnessing the death and burial of woolly mammoths.

• The evolutionary scientists especially have a problem with burial in wind-blown silt. Uniformitarian theory requires the environment to have been similar to the boggy environment of today. Evolutionary scientists cannot envision gigantic dust storms because of their stretched out time scale. Furthermore, uniformitarianism requires small dust storms that built up over long periods. Their dust storms would be too small to cover a dead mammoth before the bones turned into dust. Guthrie (1990) states:

> These [large bones] could not be preserved by a few millimeters of annual eolian loess-fall; their preservation required large quantities of reworked silt.

• To this day they are left without an adequate explanation of how this could have happened. The dust storms over their immense amount of time would be insignificant. Which time scale a person chooses makes a very significant difference in how data is interpreted. It does make a difference in solving long-standing mysteries. The short time scale of Scripture provides viable solutions to the many mysteries of the past. Telescoping the dust storms into a one-hundred or two-hundred year period at the end of the Ice Age makes the dust storms powerful enough to bury carcasses and bones rapidly.

• An Ice Age caused by the Genesis flood is able to explain the death and burial of the woolly mammoth and the wide distribution of loess, among many other puzzles. The end of the post-flood Ice Age would start with the tropics becoming warmer. The higher latitudes would be colder than they are today. The cold air and the warm air would collide and cause strong, windy dust storms. Wind-blown silt deposits are found all across the Northern Hemisphere south of where the ice sheets once existed. Dust storms at the end of the Ice Age would be so severe that they would be much worse than the Dust Bowl era experienced in the Midwest of the United States during the 1930s. During that time, the dust storms covered up fences and tractors. One storm even caused drifts as high as the roof of a farmhouse.

The "Bone" Islands

• In our story, Tungus and his ancestors saw the Arctic Ocean sometimes rising rapidly. Judging by the bone finds, millions of woolly mammoths inhabited the continental shelf and adjacent land at this time. Most of the time the rise was gradual and the animals were able to escape from drowning. Evidence indicates the sea level occasionally rose very fast. Ice-dammed lakes may have burst and flooded into the ocean. Catastrophic summer melting of the ice sheets would swell the rivers flooding into the ocean. A quick unexpected rise in sea level would catch many animals by surprise as they grazed on the nearly flat continental shelf off northern Siberia. Many mammoths sought refuge in what Tungus' tribe called the New Siberian Hills. Within a short time the hills were surrounded with water, concentrating the population. Trapped on the islands with a diminishing supply of food and water, they would die en masse. Thousands of woolly mammoth bones cover the islands. Some explorers have come back with reports that whole islands are composed of bones, but this is surely an exaggeration. Nevertheless, the bones are extremely abundant on the New Siberian Islands.

This would more logically explain the great abundance of loess in the lowlands of Siberia and Alaska.

Giant dust storms at the end of the Ice Age can also explain the carcass puzzles. Tungus' tribe told Eric's tribe about finding a woolly mammoth that was suffocated and buried during a dust storm. A woolly mammoth or any other large animal caught in a severe dust storm would put its back to the storm and try to ride it out. Its body would act as a snow fence with the dust accumulating around it. Once the woolly mammoth realized it was stuck, it would try to free itself. The stress on the limb could break a leg.

Over 50 mammoth skeletons were found trapped in a sinkhole at Hot Springs, South Dakota. Many of them had broken legs. The mammoths caught in the sinkhole most likely broke their legs trying to

extricate their forelimbs from the mud (Agenbroad and Mead, 1994).

Woolly mammoths killed in a standing position in the dust storms of Siberia would freeze quickly. The dust storm or successive dust storms would completely bury it. Cold would creep up from the permafrost, freezing its legs. Cold from the air would freeze the top of the mammoth or what was exposed. Soon the mound would become a block of ice. The animal would not need to be jammed into the permafrost, as suggested by Howorth — the permafrost would come up to meet the mammoth!

The Berezovka mammoth not only had a broken forelimb, but also broken ribs and pelvis. The pelvis and ribs could have been broken long after the animal was buried and frozen. It has been noted by Siberian scientists that permafrost can shift in a way similar to a fault in the earth's crust (Vereshchagin and Tomirdiaro, 1999). It is possible that the permafrost faulted, breaking the pelvis and ribs.

It is important to note that only a few woolly mammoths were buried in a generally standing position. The rest of the mammoth remains are bones and tusks. It appears that they died and decomposed before they became part of the permafrost. Only the most severe dust storms would suffocate a mammoth and leave it in a general standing position. Less severe dust storms would simply bury mammoths that died earlier of cold or starvation. Fewer than a hundred carcasses have been found in Siberia. Of these there are only about one or two dozen that have large pieces of preserved flesh. So, a fair conclusion would be that nearly all mammoths and other animals died by other means before they were covered with dust. Even yet, they have to have been covered fairly quickly, or the bones and tusks would have decayed. Since the bones and tusks are commonly found well-preserved, especially farther north, the dust had to have buried them within a few tens of years.

It is important to note that the abundant bone graveyards do not support a quick-freeze theory. Half digested vegetation is found in some of the Siberian and Alaskan carcasses that have been examined. The explanation is found by examining the digestive system of modern-day elephants. The elephant kind today shares the same digestive system, so it is reasonable to assume the mammoths were similar. An elephant actually digests its food after the food passes through the stomach. The stomach is mainly a holding pouch; microorganisms in the intestines, colon, and caecum do most of the digestion. The stomach environment is highly acidic. This acid would break down some of the vegetation but not totally destroy it. If the animal died before the food passed out of the stomach, it would remain there and freeze. So they do not have to be quick frozen to explain the state of the stomach vegetation. A more gradual freezing would explain it.

In Alaska, the loess deposits have slumped down into the valleys because the terrain of Alaska is hillier than Siberia. As the wind-blown silt collected on the land, it became unstable. It slid to lower levels and mixed animal bones and plants buried in the loess. This material has been called muck by the gold miners, who wash it away to find the gold in the gravel below.

End Ice Age Mass Extinction

At the end of the Ice Age the woolly mammoths, woolly rhinoceros, ground sloth, saber-toothed tiger, Irish elk, and many others went extinct. Sometimes a mammal disappeared from an entire continent. In North America, 70 percent of all large mammals over 100 pounds (45 kg) disappeared including horses and camels (Agenbroad and Nelson, 2002). This represents 100 species. Horses were introduced later by Europeans. Many large birds, mostly carrion feeders, also disappeared. Such extinctions also occurred on other continents of the world. Australia lost 90 percent of its large animals, including the giant kangaroos and wombats (Agenbroad and Nelson, 2002).

The end Ice Age extinctions are another major mystery for evolutionists during the Ice Age. At the moment there are two main explanations. They think either the climate or man (or both) caused these mass extinctions. However, there are problems with these ideas.

With the Ice Age developing after a worldwide flood, these extinctions can be explained by using Siberia as an example. Evolutionary scientists believe the winters during the Ice Age were quite cold, while it was warming up at the end of the Ice Age. In an Ice Age after the Flood, it was the opposite. Winters were mild during the Ice Age and cold at the end. When temperatures plummeted at the end of the Ice Age, the animals were severely stressed. Drier conditions caused drought, diminishing their food supply.

But, as in Siberia, we believe the key to the extinctions was the severe dust storms. Many of the mammals should have been able to handle the cold. The drought would cause a shortage of food and water. Mass death would result, especially for the larger mammals, since their needs were greater. But some animals, such as the camel, can handle drought. It is likely the severe dust storms finished the job of mass extinction, even for the camels of North America. There is abundant evidence for severe dust storms in the United States in all the wind-blown silt south of the former ice sheets.

So, the combination of cold winters, drought, and dust storms, along with predators and man, contributed to the end Ice Age mass extinctions over the earth. Once the large plant-eating animals perished, the large carnivorous mammals and birds would mostly die. Man would also have been stressed. He would have hunted large mammals. The animals would have been easy to hunt near watering holes during drought. There were many millions of large mammals and not that many people. Man could not have been responsible for the mass extinctions at the end of the Ice Age, as some evolutionists have suggested.

Questions

1) What do you think life would have been like at the very end of the Ice Age?

2) Why did a majority of large animals go extinct on all continents as the ice sheets melted?

3) Why did the woolly mammoth disappear from Siberia and become extinct?

4) Why did Ice Age people use stone spear points and stone tools?

5) Why was the Arctic Ocean warm at the beginning of the Ice Age?

6) Why were Siberian winters mild and wet early in the Ice Age?

7) Why were Siberian summers cool with little snowmelt in the mountains?

8) Why were only the mountains of Siberia glaciated during the Ice Age?

9) Why was Siberia a grassland during much of the Ice Age?

10) Why was there a worldwide flood?

11) Why did the bogs form near the end of the Ice Age?

12) What caused all the dust storms in Siberia?

13) Why did the shore of the Arctic Ocean (Lake Arctica) move north and then south during the Ice Age?

14) How did the Arctic Ocean (lake Arctica) freeze over with sea ice?

15) Why did winters become colder and summers warmer at the end of the Ice Age?

16) Where does all the snow for an ice age come from?

17) How did Noah's flood cause the Ice Age?

18) Why were some woolly mammoths found in a general standing position, suffocated and frozen in permafrost?

References

Agenbroad, L. D. and L. Nelson, 2002. *Mammoths: Ice Age Giants*, Lerner Publications Company, Minneapolis, Minnesota.

Agenbroad, L. D. and M. I. Mead, 1994. "The Taphonomy of Mammuthus Remains in a Closed System Trap, Hot Springs Mammoth Site, South Dakota," In Agenbroad, L. D. and M. I. Mead (editors), *The Hot Springs Mammoth Site, The Mammoth Site of Hot Springs, South Dakota, Rapid City, South Dakota*, p. 283-305.

Alt, D., 2001. *Glacial Lake Missoula and Its Humongous Floods*, Mountain Press Publishing Company, Missoula, Montana.

Dennell, R. W., 1992. *The Origins of Crop Agriculture in Europe*. In Cowan, C. W. and Watson, P. J. (editors), *The Origins of Agriculture — An International Perspective*, Smithsonian Institution Press, Washington, D. C., p. 71–94.

Guthrie, R. D., 1990. *Frozen Fauna of the Mammoth Steppe: The Story of Blue Babe*, University of Chicago Press, Chicago, Illinois.

Howorth, H. H., 1887. *The Mammoth and the Flood — An Attempt to Confront the Theory of Uniformity with the Facts of Recent Geology*, Sampson Low, Marston, Searle, & Rivington, London. Reproduced by The Sourcebook Project, Glen Arm, Maryland.

Lubenow, M. L., 2004. *Bones of Contention: A Creationist Assessment of Human Fossils*, Baker Book House, Grand Rapids, Michigan.

Oard, M. J., 1990. *An Ice Age Caused by the Genesis Flood*, Institute for Creation Research, El Cajon, California.

Oard, M. J., 2004a. *The Lake Missoula Flood Controversy and the Genesis Flood*, Creation Research Society Monograph 13, Chino Valley, Arizona.

Oard, M. J., 2004b. *Frozen in Time: The Woolly Mammoth, the Ice Age and the Bible*. Master Books, Green Forest, Arkansas.

Oard, M. J., 2005. *The Frozen Record: Examining the Ice Core History of the Greenland and Antarctic Ice Sheets*, Institute for Creation Research, El Cajon, California.

Oard, M. J. and B. Oard, 1993. *Life in the Great Ice Age*, Master Books, Green Forest, Arkansas.

Pfizenmayer, E. W., 1939, *Siberian Man and Mammoth*, Blackie & Sons, London.

Pitulko, V. V., P. A. Nilolsky, E. Yu. Girya, A. E. Basilyan, V. E. Tumskoy, S. A. Koulakov, S. N. Astakhov, E. Yu. Pavlova, and M. A. Anisimov, 2004. "The Yana RHS Site: Humans in the Arctic before the Last Glacial Maximum," *Science* 303:52-56.

Scarre, C., 1998. *Exploring Prehistoric Europe*, Oxford University Press, New York.

Stone, R., 2004. "A Surprising Survival Story in the Siberian Arctic", *Science* 303:33.

Tolmachoff, I. P., 1929. *The Carcasses of the Mammoth and Rhinoceros in the Frozen Ground of Siberia*, Transactions of the American Philosophical Society 23:11-74.

Vereshchagin, N. K. and S. V. Tomirdiaro, 1999. "Taphonomic Research in the Permafrost Regions: A Survey of Past and Present Studies in the Former Soviet Union." In Haynes, G., J. Klimowicz, and J. W. F. Reumer, (editors), *Mammoths and the Mammoth Fauna: Studies of an Extinct Ecosystem*, Proceedings of the First International Mammoth Conference, Jaarbericht Van Het Natuurmuseum, Rotterdam, p. 87-198.

Ward, P. D., 1997. *Call of the Distant Mammoths — Why the Ice Age Mammoths Disappeared*, Springer-Verlag, New York.

Watson, T., 1997. "What Causes Ice Ages?" *U.S. News & World Report*, 123(7):58–60.

Woodmorappe, J., 1996. *Noah's Ark: A Feasibility Study*, Institute for Creation Research, El Cajon, California.

Glossary

Amulet — something worn, often around the neck, as supposed protection against injury or evil.

Animal husbandry — the process of caring for and raising of animals for food.

Anthropology — the study of man.

Archaeology — the scientific study of the life and culture of ancient peoples.

Astronomical theory of the ice age or ages — the theory that small changes in the earth's orbital configuration around the sun caused ice ages.

Beetle-Brow people — the Neaderthal people, a family of humans, who arrived in the area before and interacted with Lathan's tribe.

Bering Land Bridge — the land connection between northeast Asia and Alaska during the Ice Age.

Black Lake — Ice Age man's term for the Black Sea.

Caecum — the pouch which is the beginning of the large intestine.

Civilization — the process of becoming civilized and gathering into social organizations.

Colon — that part of the large intestine extending from the caecum to the anus.

Continental Europe — that part of the European continent south of the United Kingdom (Ireland, Scotland, Wales, and England) and Scandinavia (mainly Norway, Sweden, and Finland).

Continental shelf — the submerged shelf of land that slopes gradually from the shoreline to the steep descent called the continental slope.

Cro-Magnon people — people who came after the Neaderthal people and lived in Europe during the Ice Age with the Neaderthals. They probably represent the modern Europeans. Erik's tribe was part of the Cro-Magnon people.

Deglaciation phase of Ice Age — the melting of the ice sheets at the end of the Ice Age.

Dust storms — wind storms that pick up dust from the ground into the air.

Evaporation — the process of liquid water changing into water vapor.

Extinction — the disappearance of an animal or plant species from the earth.

Geometric Progression — a sequence of numbers in which the ratio of each number to the preceding one is the same throughout the sequence, for example, 1, 2, 4, 8, 16, 32, etc.

Glacial period — the part of the Ice Age dominated by ice sheets, according to evolutionary terminology.

Glacial till — rocks of all sizes within a finer-grained matrix around the rocks that were deposited by a glacier or ice sheet.

Glacier — a large mass of ice and snow.

Great Flood — Noah's flood.

Great forest of Siberia — the widespread forests south of the tundra.

Great Ice Age — the term used in the story for the single Ice Age that occurred rapidly within a period of about 700 years following the Flood.

Great wall of ice — the edge of the ice sheet.

Hunter-gatherers — people who live by hunting and gathering food, like berries or roots, from the land.

Ice core — a tube of ice drilled from a glacier or ice sheet.

Ice free path or corridor — a slot along the eastern slopes of the Rocky Mountains in western Canada and Montana between the ice sheet over the western mountains and that over central and eastern Canada.

Ice lenses — lenses of ice that form in permafrost.

Ice sheet — a large mass of ice and snow.

Ice wedge — a wedge shaped mass of ice that forms down from the surface of permafrost.

Interglacial period — the part of an Ice Age in which the ice sheets melt away, according to evolutionary terminology.

Intestine — the lower part of the alimentary canal extending from the stomach to the anus.

Javelin — a light spear for throwing.

Koumiss — fermented reindeer milk.

Lake Arctica — Ice Age man's term for the Arctic Ocean.

Lake Baltica — Ice Age man's term for the Baltic Sea, north of continental Europe.

Lake Pacifica — Ice Age man's term for the Pacific Ocean.

Lateral moraine — a moraine formed when rocks and finer particles from a glacier were dumped to the sides of a glacier.

Legume — any of a large group of plants of the pea family.

Lentil — a plant of the pea family.

Loess — wind-blown silt, especially during the Ice Age.

Moraine — a mound of rocks and fine-grained sediment left from a glacier or ice sheet.

Moon time — ancient way of counting time by the periods of the moon and the number of cycles.

Mutation — a change in the genes of an organism.

New Siberian Islands — Islands in the Arctic Ocean northeast of the Lena River delta. The islands would be hills when the Arctic continental shelf was exposed.

Nomads — people that wander from place to place.

North Star, direction of — Ice Age man's way of saying north.

Overflow — the act of a river or stream when it rises and spreads out of its banks.

Paleontology — the study of fossils.

Paleozoology — the study of ancient animals.

Permafrost — permanently frozen ground.

Poultice — a soft, moist mass applied to a sore or cut.

Prehistory — an evolutionary term meaning before recorded history. According to biblical history, there is no such thing as prehistory on earth.

Red deer — a particular species of deer.

Rising sun, direction of — Ice Age man's way of saying east.

Scandinavian Ice Sheet — the ice sheet that occupied northern Europe, northwest Asia, and some of the high mountain ranges of those continents.

Scraper — a stone tool designed for scraping.

Setting sun, direction of — Ice Age man's way of saying west.

Shining Mountains — Tien Shan Mountains of central Asia.

Shiny rocks — rocks with metal in them that can be used for metal tools.

Sledge — a sled or sleigh for carrying passengers or loads over ice and snow.

Smelting ore — the act of melting ore to collect the metal.

Terminal or end moraine — a moraine formed when rocks and finer particles from a glacier were dumped in front of a glacier.

Thaw — the warming up and melting of snow.

Uniformitarianism — the doctrine of geology that assumes present processes can explain all the rocks and fossils formed in the past.

Wind-blown silt — silt-sized particles that are blown by the wind into heaps.

Index

Our Award-Winning
Wonders of Creation Series

Filled with special features, every exciting title includes over 200 beautiful full-color photos and illustrations, practical hands-on learning experiments, charts, graphs, glossary, and index — it's no wonder these books have become one of our most requested series.

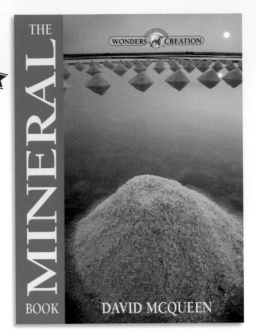

- **The Mineral Book*** reveals the first mention of minerals in the Bible and their value in culture and society.
- **The Ecology Book*** researches the relationship between living organisms and our place in God's wondrous creation.
- **The Archaeology Book*** uncovers ancient history from alphabets to ziggurats.
- **The Cave Book** digs deep into the hidden wonders beneath the surface.
- **The New Astronomy Book*** soars through the solar system separating myth from fact.
- **The Geology Book** provides a tour of the earth's crust pointing out the beauty and the scientific evidences for creation.
- **The Fossil Book** explains everything about fossils while also demonstrating the shortcomings of the evolutionary theory.
- **The New Ocean Book*** explores the depths of the ocean to find the mysteries of the deep.
- **The New Weather Book*** delves into all weather phenomena, including modern questions of supposed climate change.

*This title is color-coded with three educational levels in mind: 5th to 6th grades, 7th to 8th grades, and 9th through 11th grades.

8 1/2 x 11 • Casebound • 96 pages • Full-color interior
ISBN-13: 978-0-89051-802-1
JR. HIGH to HIGH SCHOOL

sample interior from The Archaeology Book

The Ecology Book
ISBN-13: 978-0-89051-701-7

The Archaeology Book
ISBN-13: 978-0-89051-573-0

The New Ocean Book
ISBN-13: 978-0-89051-905-9

The Geology Book
ISBN-13: 978-0-89051-281-4

The New Weather Book
ISBN-13: 978-0-89051-861-8

The New Astronomy Book
ISBN-13: 978-0-89051-834-2

The Fossil Book
ISBN-13: 978-0-89051-438-2

The Cave Book
ISBN-13: 978-0-89051-496-2

ELEMENTARY PALEONTOLOGY

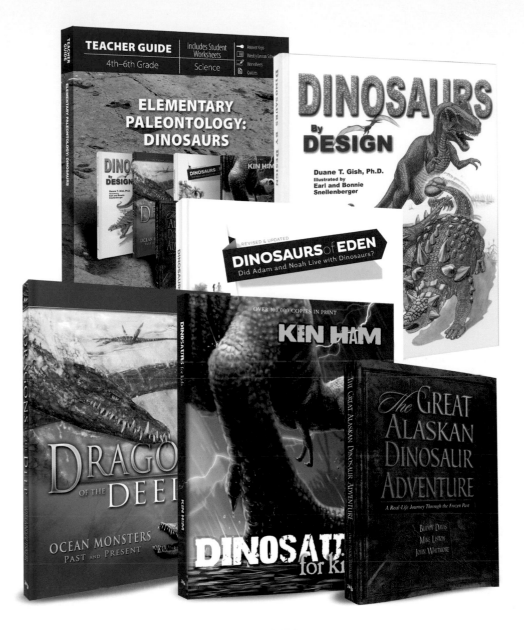

ELEMENTARY PALEONTOLOGY: DINOSAURS
GRADE 4-6

Step back in time (but not too far!) and enter the fascinating world of dinosaurs. Learn about the different kinds of dinosaurs, what they ate, when they lived, what happened to them, and more. You'll even discover that dinosaurs and people lived together!

Dinosaurs for Kids   Dinosaurs of Eden   Dinosaurs by Design   Dragons of the Deep

The Great Alaskan Dinosaur Adventure   Dinosaurs Teacher Guide

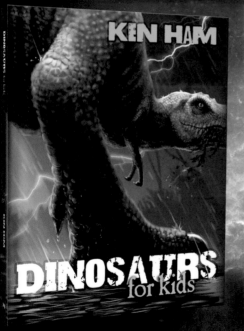

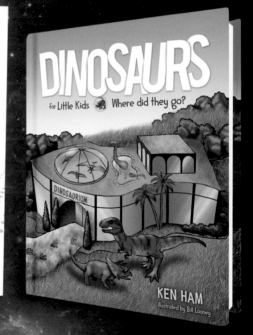

DINOSAURS FOR KIDS
Ken Ham

Within these pages kids will uncover the facts about dinosaur history from the creation to recent discoveries. Let Ken Ham take you on a journey through time to explore these awesome wonders of God's design.

978-0-89051-555-6

DINOSAURS OF EDEN
Ken Ham

Fully revised and updated, this beloved classic will take you on a breathtaking trip across time to the biblical foundation of dinosaurs. This captivating adventure by Ken Ham explores the Garden of Eden, the exciting days of Noah's Flood, and the Tower of Babel. You'll learn the true history of the earth, and discover the very meaning and purpose of life!

978-0-89051-902-8

DINOSAURS FOR LITTLE KIDS
Ken Ham

Learn the truth about the history of dinosaurs in a wonderful book designed just for little children. Explore different kinds of dinosaurs, see when they were created, and why they no longer roam the world today!

978-1-68344-199-1

Available where fine books are sold.   MasterBooks.com

Answers

1) Winters would become colder, summers warmer, and the air drier, with less precipitation. Dust storms would have been frequent. It was now possible to leave the caves in northern Europe and live in manmade dwellings, but conditions would have been very harsh in northern Siberia. Civilization in Europe could start with the building of shelters, planting of crops in the summer, domesticating animals, and smelting metals.

2) Winters became much colder, the climate drier with drought, and dust storms became frequent and severe.

3) The woolly mammoth was stressed by colder winters, increasing permafrost and bogs, flooded rivers in summer due to rapid ice melt, drought, and especially by dust storms.

4) Their metal tools wore out and could not be replaced as they spread from the Tower of Babel region.

5) Because of the breaking up of the "Fountains of the Great Deep," and the volcanic lava flows resulting in warm ocean water, pole to pole and surface to ocean depths, immediately after the Flood.

6) Because of onshore flow of mild air heated by the warm Arctic and North Pacific oceans. More rapid evaporation from the high latitude oceans would produce more precipitation. More winter condensation of water vapor would add more heat of condensation to the atmosphere.

7) Because of volcanic ash and gases trapped in the stratosphere, reflecting more sunlight back to space. Less sunlight absorbed on the ground results in less summer heating.

8) Summers were still warm enough to melt the winter snow at low elevations, but not in the mountains.

9) As the Ice Age progressed and the oceans cooled off, winters would become cooler and drier with less snow. The Scandinavian Ice Sheet to the west would cause a downslope warming and drying effect in northern Siberia. The drier climate with a lack of permafrost would result in a grassland and be more unfavorable to trees.

10) Because Genesis chapter 6:5 states "…that the wickedness of man was great on the earth, and that every intent of the thoughts of his heart was only evil continually" (NASB).

11) Bogs form because of the melting of the top one or two feet (about 0.5 m) of permafrost during summer. Permafrost forms by the cooling of the air during winter. Mild winters at first would give way to colder winters later in the Ice Age, causing permafrost.

12) Dust storms would be caused by greater wind and drier air at the end of the Ice Age.

13) As more snow and ice accumulated in ice sheets, sea level would fall and the shoreline of the Arctic Ocean would move north. When the ice sheets melted, the opposite happened.

14) Seawater is difficult to freeze, but when the ice caps over the mountains melted at the end of the Ice Age, fresh water of less density spread over the salty Arctic Ocean. Fresh water is much easier to freeze.

15) Winters became cooler because of colder ocean water resulting in colder air, less evaporation with less release of heat of condensation, and more sea ice. Summers became warmer because of more sunshine as volcanic ash and gases decreased.

16) The snow comes mostly from all the water evaporated from the warm ocean at mid and high latitude. The warmer the ocean surface, the more the evaporation and snow.

17) The Flood caused much more volcanism during and afterwards. Greater volcanism caused more reflection of sunlight and cooler summers. The Flood also caused warm mid and high latitude oceans that resulted in much greater evaporation and snowfall.

18) Because some woolly mammoths were caught in severe dust storms. The dust would pile around them, like snow around a snow fence. This would cause them to suffocate and end up in a general standing position. The dust froze and became part of the permafrost.